SELF-CONSCIOUSNESS
SELF-TREATED

WORKS BY A. A. ROBACK

THE INTERFERENCE OF WILL-IMPULSES. 166 pp. — $2.75
BEHAVIORISM AND PSYCHOLOGY. 285 pp. — Out of Print.
PSYCHOLOGY WITH CHAPTERS ON CHARACTER ANALYSIS AND MENTAL MEASUREMENT. Out of Print.
ROBACK MENTALITY TESTS FOR SUPERIOR ADULTS (8th edition). COMPREHENSION TESTS (3d ed.), SCIENTIFIC INGENUITY AND JURISTIC APTITUDE TESTS. $2.00 Sample Set. (Manuals: 75c; 50c; $2.25)
THE PSYCHOLOGY OF CHARACTER. (3d rev. and enlarged ed.), 794 pp. — $8.00
PISCOLOGIA DEL CARACTER. (Madrid), 654 pp. — $6.00
A BIBLIOGRAPHY OF CHARACTER AND PERSONALITY. 340 pp. — $4.00
POPULAR PSYCHOLOGY. Illustrated. (Out of Print), 267 pp.
JEWISH INFLUENCE IN MODERN THOUGHT. 506 pp., illustrated — $4.50
PERSONALITY: THE CRUX OF SOCIAL INTERCOURSE (o.p.)
BUSINESS PSYCHOLOGY. (Correspondence Course), Eight Booklets for Commonwealth of Massachusetts
SELF-CONSCIOUSNESS, SELF-TREATED. 265 pp. (2d ed. in press)
VARFOR HAMMAR JAG MIG SJALV, (Swedish translation of above), 160 pages (Stockholm) — $2.50
CURIOSITIES OF YIDDISH LITERATURE. 227 pp. (Out of Print)
I. L. PERETZ: PSYCHOLOGIST OF LITERATURE. 458 pp. — $4.00
BEHAVIORISM AT 25. 256 pp. (Out of Print)
THE PSYCHOLOGY OF COMMON SENSE. 350 pp. — $3.80
SENSE OF HUMOR TEST. (2d ed.) 50 cents
THE STORY OF YIDDISH LITERATURE. (Illustrated) 510 pp. — $5.00
APOLOGIA PRO VITA YIDDICIA. 98 pp. — $1.50 (300 numbered copies)
WILLIAM JAMES. (500 numbered copies), 340 pp. — $4.00
A DICTIONARY OF INTERNATIONAL SLURS. 394 pp. — $6.25
PSYCHORAMA; A PSYCHOLOGICAL ANALYSIS. 365 pp. — $3.75
PERSONALITY: In Theory and Practice. 438 pp.—$4.50

EDITED

PROBLEMS OF PERSONALITY. (Second ed.), 443 pp. — $7.00

Collected papers of the late Dr. Morton Prince, under the title of
CLINICAL AND EXPERIMENTAL STUDIES IN PERSONALITY
672 pages (2d revised and enlarged edition)— (de luxe) $12.50

THE ALBERT SCHWEITZER JUBILEE BOOK. 508 pp. — $7.50
HANNS SACHS'S MASKS OF LOVE AND LIFE. 306 pp. — $4.25

TRANSLATED AND EDITED
(With Introduction and 169 Notes)

BASTIAT-SCHULZE VON DELITZSCH (F. Lassalle), 434 pp. — (Out of Print)

POPULAR PAMPHLETS ON PERSONALITY AND FOLKLORE
(some illustrated with many cuts)

Improving Your Personality
Readings For Cultural Personality
"I Am Winning Friends"
On Reading Character
Psychological Aspects of Jewish Protective Phrases
Physicians in Jewish Folklore

The Yiddish Proverb
Getting More Out of Life
Success in Handling Types
Overcoming Inferiority Complexes
Personality in Handwriting
The Use and Meaning of Dreams
The Psychology of Confession

SELF-CONSCIOUSNESS
SELF-TREATED

By

A. A. ROBACK

*Professor of Psychology, Emerson College
Formerly Professor of Psychology and English,
Northeastern University and Instructor at Harvard
University; Sometime National Research Council Fellow
in the Biological Sciences*

SCI-ART PUBLISHERS
HARVARD SQUARE
CAMBRIDGE, MASSACHUSETTS

THE MURRAY PRINTING COMPANY, WAKEFIELD, MASSACHUSETTS

*DEDICATED TO THE MILLIONS OF SENSITIVE SOULS
WHO HAVE LOST THE OPPORTUNITIES SNATCHED AT
BY THEIR TOUGH-MINDED BROTHERS AND SISTERS,
BUT HAVE FOUND THEMSELVES IN THIS VERY LOSS.*

PREFACE

It is perhaps not strange that a book on self-consciousness should be in constant demand, particularly as there are no other books on the subject available. When the whole edition of *Self-Consciousness and Its Treatment,* which was published in 1931, became exhausted, I thought it would be best to re-write a good part of the material and add to it, so that it could be of greater help to readers who were troubled with self-consciousness. The result has been the present volume, which contains about twice as much matter as its predecessor.

To one or two of the reviewers of *Self-Consciousness and Its Treatment,* there seemed to be a question as to whether the book was written for psychologists and psychiatrists or for lay people who needed the information for themselves. The present title, while not excluding the professional class, at any rate indicates that the exposition is such as would be accessible to the non-professional.

SELF-CONSCIOUSNESS SELF-TREATED

It is not necessary to assume that books, on ordinary subjects at least, must be written either for the classes or the masses. There is no reason why an academic person might not benefit from a popularly written book; and again there is still less reason for a layman to throw up his hands when a book contains a dozen terms for which a large dictionary must be consulted. If a discussion or presentation is clear and direct, it should be understood by every one with ordinary intelligence; and if it is sound and solid, it should be of benefit to those professionals who are interested in that particular subject. Let us recall that Darwin's epoch-making works could be enjoyed by workingmen who had received no higher education; and men like Helmholtz, Mach, Boole, Max Müller and numerous other scientists of a high order have been excellent popularizers.

The ancient Egyptians, as is well known, had a *demotic* form of writing for the people, and a *hieratic* form for the priests. During the Middle Ages and Renaissance, the vernacular was used for the untutored and Latin for the

PREFACE

learned. While we have done away with the double set of characters and bi-lingualism in approaching the mere reader and the exalted scholar, we still have retained the doubleness in mental attitude and vocabulary or syntax, with the result that academic and professional treatises become more and more technical, while books written for *hoi polloi* degenerate into a conglomeration of half-truths, garnished with slang phrases, wisecracks and oft-repeated platitudes. Thus the scientist begins to shun everything which is not stated in almost quantitative language, while the lay public is bored by anything which does not make use of inspirational "pep" talks, interlarded with stories from the screen, diamond, gridiron or mat heroes.

The present little work is addressed to every intelligent person who has some concern in the subject. The psychologist or psychiatrist will, of course, be able to take it at a hurried tempo, while the "running" reader may need to retard his pace. The facts are not different for the two categories of readers; and the training of one individual is sometimes compensated for by the insight or understanding of another.

In attempting to cover all the phases of self-consciousness, I have not tried to deal exhaustively with any one situation or introduce what might be considered irrelevant matter only to satisfy some particular hypothesis. One appreciative critic, of the psychoanalytic camp, naturally thought that I should have regarded self-consciousness exclusively as an expression of narcissism, and incidentally took exception to the statement that there was a decided lack of literature on the subject; for, according to his contention, the disguises of self-consciousness in one form or another have been amply treated by psychoanalysts.

My reply is that, of self-consciousness the sufferer is quite certain, while the alleged unconscious sources of self-consciousness he is not sure about; nor are we, for that matter. However narcissism may be related to the state of mind under study, it is not identical. Similarly the cavilling critic—the only one I am glad to say—who thought I did not go into the "distortion of values, inadequate conditioning, over-suppression,'' did not take the trouble to perceive that I had given all these causes an honorable mention, without awarding the prize to any particular one. Inadequate conditioning may be a good explanation, displacement, even better; narcissism, oversuppression, and whatnot, play their part, but in the last analysis it is common sense which helps us to evaluate these factors in their etiological perspective. If, then, I did not veer too much from that touchstone of science, I can consider myself well acquitted.

The title of this book needs a word of defence. If we assume that self-consciousness is due to some Freudian mechanism or to wrong conditioning, the implication that self-consciousness does not require the assistance of a psychologist, psychoanalyst or psychiatrist must fall. I too believe that in obstinate cases, in the morbid forms of self-consciousness, a specialist must be called in. I shall even go further and admit that in ordinary cases of self-consciousness, treatment, in the form of

conferences or analysis by trained men, will
benefit the troubled individual, but there is no
reason to suppose that one cannot endeavor to
cure himself of this trait by dint of hard work:
first learning the causes, both general and
specific, and then making every effort to change
one's point of view and, through practice and
discipline, breaking the resistance and inhibitions which all self-conscious people are guilty
of encouraging in themselves.

There was a time when physicians of the
mind were an idea of the future. The neurotics
of a century ago had to shift for themselves or
look to the priest for solace. The stronger
minds turned physicians and took themselves in
hand. The most striking example of these self-
disciplined men is Immanuel Kant, celebrated
for his three *Critiques* but perhaps equally
great for his mastery of fate. What we loosely
call "nervousness" today did not spare the
constitution of the Copernicus of modern philosophy. He had consulted his friend Markus
Herz about his physical ailments, but there
was no one he could resort to in connection with
his depressed moods, to which he, like ordi-

nary mortals, must have been subject, in consequence particularly of the terrific strain that
he had undergone while formulating the system
of philosophy which is the only one that is still
alive in the universities of the world. The philosopher, we find, is forced to become a psychiatrist; and he writes his remarkable essay
*The Power of the Mind, through Sheer Deter-
mination to Become Master Over Morbid Feelings*—a little treatise which may be looked upon
as a forerunner of the modern conceptions of
suggestion and auto-suggestion.

Of course it will be retorted that we cannot
all be like Kant; and, besides, conditions have
changed since. Even in organic ailments, a
physician calls in another physician to treat his
case. It is very unusual for a surgeon to operate on himself or even his kin. The contention of psychoanalysis has been that no one can
analyze himself, since the resistance which our
unconscious exercises will interfere with our
perception. Even conservative psychology
recognizes the individual blind spot, the personal equation, or whatever you wish to call the

differential which prevents our seeing things in an objective light.

Conceding all this and more—the attitude adopted by Kant must still gain our approbation and even admiration. There are certain mental quirks which require treatment from without. Ordinary self-consciousness is not one of them. So long as the method of examining oneself is supplied, the patient may proceed to write his own prescription, varying it according to the circumstances. The treatment here amounts to a revaluation of social situations, an understanding of oneself, a re-education of one's point of view, and consequently a changed attitude toward the world. The rest follows as "night follows the day."

It is not to be gathered that the same method can be recommended for the treatment of phobias, obsessions, and other psychoneuroses. Fortunately self-consciousness, unless of the severer variety, is not in the same class and may well be treated by the "patient," by readjusting his behavior and modifying his outlook on life.

June 27, 1936.   A. A. ROBACK.

PREFACE

To the Lay Reader

Since a great many who are beset by self-consciousness did not enjoy a good education, this being one of the causes of the tendency, it seems advisable to say a few words to them in connection with the use of this book. I had intended making certain recommendations in the general preface but it occurred to me that such readers are too impatient to read the preface, in which case the situation would resemble a sign being placed at the foot of a mountain road, reading "Those who cannot read this sign must take the road at the extreme right."

The average reader will probably be eager to plunge into the midst of things and wish to discover immediately the remedy for self-consciousness. To such, part of the first chapter will be irksome; hence pages 25-34 should be either omitted or read toward the last. The logical development of the subject requires this chapter at the beginning, but it may be dispensed with if the materials sounds a bit advanced. Another part which may call for a certain amount of training is Chapter X, on the dynamic theories. Yet it is surprising what a careful reading and re-reading will do to broaden one's horizon along this line.

Naturally in several other chapters there will occur words, phrases, sentences and even paragraphs which to a beginner will not be altogether familiar. But the dictionary is a great help on such occasions, and there is no reason why the uneducated should use the dictionary less than the educated. Sometimes, too, a friend may be asked to explain a statement that is not clear. It is just a step of this sort which will have its beneficial effect in one's self-treatment. That one type of endeavor is bound up with the other hardly needs any proof. It is characteristic for an executive of high standing to seek information from anyone. He will not be ashamed to order a copy of a book on personality, self-consciousness, inferiority complexes, etc. The average self-conscious person, however, is fearful lest some one of his friends might learn that he is reading such a book. It is an irony that those who have gone a long way toward self-improvement are ready to continue their quest, and will not fear the idea of exposing themselves to the banter of acquaintances, while those who cannot afford to lose opportunities of correcting personality faults will be deterred by what Tom, Dick and Harry, whose thoughts are of no account, may think of them.

The reader should be warned against picking out a paragraph or even a chapter here and there. Continuity is essential in understanding the main issues; and this little book was not written for the lazy reader. No matter how difficult a passage seems to be, the person who applies himself, though practically uneducated, will master it and as he overcomes his difficulties in the exposition, his self-assurance will grow, and with it, his self-consciousness is bound to wane.

It is in deference to the needs of the somewhat uncultivated reader that I have for once brought myself to give a summary of the book (Chapter XIV) irksome as repetition is for me in any form. Most likely this recapitulation will be regarded by a goodly number of readers as the most accessible, and therefore most serviceable, portion of the volume, but it would be a mistake to be contented with a mere résumé, when an understanding of the whole subject is necessary.

A. A. R.

Cambridge, Mass.

CONTENTS

Philosophical Sense—Dialectic Fly Paper—
Psychological Approach — The Genetic
Phase—The Popular Meaning of Self-Consciousness—Popular Meaning of the Term
Adopted in Literature—Universal Life Problem—Ego-Consciousness to Refer to Undue
Self-Regard—The Two Terms Denote Opposite Urges.

Dearth of Literature — A Statistical Surprise — Adults Do Not Appear Self-Conscious—Chronic and Acute Self-Consciousness.

How Does It Feel to Be Self-Conscious?—
Objective Symptoms—Classic Description of
Embarrassment—Recovering from Embarrassment—Phases of Self-Consciousness.

A Task Requires Thousands of Nerve Operations—Nerves Are Thrown Out of Gear—
The Self and Work Interfere—Self Interferes
with Automatic Working of Act—The Fear
Element in Self-Consciousness—Physiological
Locus—Are the Glands Involved?

CONTENTS

CONTENTS

CONTENTS

CONTENTS

[21]

SELF-CONSCIOUSNESS
SELF-TREATED

CHAPTER I

DIFFERENT SENSES OF SELF-CONSCIOUSNESS

When I started to write the predecessor of this little book, a colleague of mine happened to ask me what I was working on. "Self-Consciousness," I say.

"Self-consciousness?" he asks somewhat surprised. "That will take you back into quite a philosophical maze, but what will be your experimental controls?"

I realized then and there that my colleague and I were talking two different languages, or at any rate, that we were using the term *self-consciousness* in two different senses; for it had not occurred to me that self-consciousness had any more of a history than a headache or a common cold.

We all know that a word means different things to different people, depending on their interests, experiences, environment, desires, etc. A case to a physician is not quite the same as a case to the lawyer, and a lawyer's case is again a far cry from the social worker's case. To a liquor merchant or a bootlegger a case means something different again. Why then assume that self-consciousness applies to just one thing?

Before we go any farther, then, it is essential that our topic be set in its proper context, otherwise the issues will necessarily be mixed.

Philosophical Sense

To the philosopher and laboratory psychologist, particularly of the structural school, self-consciousness means the act or condition of being (or the process of becoming) directly aware of the self or ego during any mental process, or in other words, awareness of what we experience as relating to a self as the subject of these experiences. The theoretical question of self-consciousness has been debated back and forth in philosophical treatises for many a decade. Kant's synthetic unity of apperception was a bomb which reverberated in many lands, everywhere precipitating a can-

nonade that was to make the philosophical
world safe for logomachy, that is to say, the
battle of words.

To the layman it may sound strange that the
most profound, or perhaps only abstruse philosophers, dealt with the problem of self-consciousness in their own way. Fichte, the succes-
sor of Kant in philosophical leadership, was so
preoccupied with the "ego" or "I" or "self,"
that he appeared to entertain the belief that
before we had an awareness of our own "I,"
the world did not exist for us. In fact I retain the impression from my student days that
somewhere in his *Wissenschaftslehre* (The
Science of Knowledge) he makes the bold
assertion that a child does not exist until
it has become self-conscious. If for Fichte,
who did not write for the masses or even the
general reading public, life does not begin at
forty, he might nevertheless have been the first
to recognize that existence and life are not the
same; and like every idealist would insist on
putting all stress on consciousness, ideas, mind.

Hegel, for a century the oracle of idealists in

philosophy, took hundreds of pages in his *Phenomenology of Mind* to explain the difference between consciousness and self-consciousness, but I doubt very much that my readers would make much headway in following him out of the maze of verbiage, which has given rise to commentaries, expositions, elucidations, but as has been said about Professor McTaggart who has written a large work entitled *"The Secret of Hegel"*—"He seems to have guarded the secret only too well."

As Hegel defines self-consciousness, it "exists in itself and for itself, in that and by the fact that it exists for another self-consciousness; that is to say, it *is* only by being acknowledged or 'recognized.' "[1]

It is not, however, among German idealists alone that the term self-consciousness is fraught with a meaning foreign to the man in the street.

Certainly when Bertrand Russell, one of the clearest thinkers of our generation, observed "This kind of acquaintance, which may be

---

[1] G. F. Hegel: *Phenomenology of Mind* (English trans. Vol. I., p. 175).

called self-consciousness, is the source of all our knowledge of mental things,'"[2] he was not using the term in the sense which the average person in the street knows it.

Dialectic Fly Paper

As an instance of the philosophical *reductio ad absurdum* hair-splitting that has been undertaken by a writer who has given us, ironically enough, *A Critique of Pure Kant,* we may treat the reader to the following abracadabra of C. K. Wheeler taken from his *The Autobiography of the I or Ego,* which is repeated in all sorts of variants by way of elucidation, and which seems to anticipate Gertrude Stein's sound acrobatics.

> Here, to begin with, is this theorem, one demonstrable, the theorem, to wit, *that the self-consciousness*—self-consciousness as such (consciousness of self *as* self)—*of the conscious self, the self something distinct from consciousness and back of it, but as having con-*

---

[2] Bertrand Russell: *The Problems of Philosophy,* p. 77.

*sciousness or being conscious, is not
only utterly unthinkable, but absolutely impossible.*

And here, following, is the demon-
stration:

Thus, it is, of course, only self-evident that there can be no self-consciousness of a thing not, itself, conscious. But, if there can be no self-
consciousness of a thing not, itself,
conscious, or until it is conscious,
then, *once* it is conscious, there can be
no self-consciousness but of what was
in the *consciousness* of the thing simply conscious. And, as what was in
the consciousness of the latter or the
conscious self, the self not consciousness itself, yet, however, that something having consciousness or being
conscious, was nothing of consciousness of that self (or it would be *already* self-conscious) nothing of that
self even, much less of that self as
such, then in the any self-consciousness as of such conscious self, there
could be nothing either of consciousness of that self as such, nor even,
indeed, of what was that self merely.

[30]

That is, the self as something distinct
from consciousness, *not being in the
consciousness of the conscious self,
would be utterly beyond the reach of
any act of self-consciousness.* So, that
the self-consciousness as such of the
self of the conscious self, the self as
something distinct from consciousness
but as having consciousness or being
conscious, is demonstrable, and here
demonstrated, an absolute impossibility; and only the self-consciousness
as such, of consciousness with its content other than self as distinct from
consciousness itself, is possible, even
if, indeed, that, even that be possible.

To state it again, that it, without
failure, be seen that there is no escape
from this,—to state it again and thus:
—Assume the self as something distinct from consciousness. If that self
be not conscious, it will be allowed only
self-evident that it could not be *self-
conscious.* Assume it, then, yet that
not consciousness itself, still as having
consciousness or being conscious; then
the *consciousness* of such conscious
self could have nothing in it of *con-*

sciousness of such self—otherwise, it would be *already* self-conscious.[3]

Pages and pages of this stuff are to be found in Wheeler's book, but this sample is enough; and every reader will probably agree that this is a word-salad, which is frequently found in the productions of senility, but some philosophers persistently indulge in such repasts.

Psychological Approach

Through Wundt, the German founder of modern psychology as a science, James, the American Dean of psychologists, and Külpe, head of the Würzburg school, the dispute between the "I" and the states of the "Me" was taken over into psychology, with self-consciousness as the crux of the issue. If there is no permanent "I," then how can one state of the mind know another, compare, judge, nay, even remember? And the postulation of a permanent "I," comes perilously close to hypothe-

---

[3] C. K. Wheeler: *The Autobiography of the I or Ego or the Metaphysics of an Interloper and Impostor Himself in the Rôle of Confessor, pp.* 19–21.

cating the existence of a soul, which to many, if not most, psychologists is an awkward predicament to be in. To some psychologists, like the late Mary Calkins, self-consciousness is pivotal in the structure of the mental sciences.

This approach to the subject is purely abstract, speculative, and even metaphysical, and need not detain us for another instant in a discussion of a practical nature.

The Genetic Phase

There is a more interesting phase of the problem of self-consciousness, and that is the *genetic* aspect with sociological implications, the general question being: In what period of the individual's life or, for that matter, in the history of the race does self-consciousness appear, and what is its process of growth? When does a child become aware of its own self as distinct from others? Are animals conscious of themselves, or only of their particular discrete experiences? Experiments on apes, in which mirrors were used, proved that primates at least can become self-conscious under suitable conditions. It is doubtful whether cats and dogs can ever be taught to regard their own reflection in the mirror or in the water as anything but the body of another cat or dog.

Bertrand Russell, indeed, thinks it "natural to suppose that self-consciousness is one of the things that distinguish men from animals: animals, we may suppose, though they have acquaintance with sense-data never become aware of this acquaintance and thus never know of their own existence."

As to the idea primitive man, or as the uneducated think of him, the savage has of his own self, there are many almost incredible stories told by specialists in that field of anthropology, relating to the curious blunders and ignorance of many tribes with regard to the self, to the extent, for example of not associating a headache with one's own head.

Of greater import is the point at which the child becomes self-conscious. Hadfield thinks that this stage in its life which in effect means that the child had learnt to distinguish between right and wrong and, therefore, has been "driven out of the garden of innocence, never to return," is the most significant fact of life in the individual.[4]

Many will be surprised to learn that this happens at the tender age of three. Psychoanalysis teaches that practically everything which befalls a person in later life derives its energy from what has taken place in these early years of formation—another version of the old saying, "The child is father to the man."

The Popular Meaning of Self-Consciousness

All that may be very interesting, but we have to consider a far more important approach to the term "self-consciousness," important, that is, from the humanistic angle. It is the layman's approach. It concerns people of every class and rank, and more particularly the average person and therefore, should not be beyond the ken or purview of science. Why this angle of the subject should be so snubbed or slurred is not readily to be accounted for, ex-

---

[4] J. A. Hadfield; *Psychology and Morals*, p. 102.

cept perhaps through the law of inertia in the academic sphere, but the fact remains that even the authoritative *Psychological Dictionary,* which appeared in 1934, defines self-consciousness as the "awareness of one's own existence and activities, usually in relation to other individuals or objects" and only in a secondary ("popular") sense translatès the word into "embarrassment," which is scarcely accurate. We may perhaps distinguish between the philosophical and the social senses of self-consciousness; and it is the latter that this book treats of. In this social or popular usage, self-consciousness denotes *preoccupation with one's own personality to such an extent as to suppose that one is the object of observation by others.*

Popular Meaning of the Term Adopted in Literature

One may call this sense of self-consciousness derived, popular, or loose, but the fact remains that it is the most vital sense, being bound up with the weal and woe of millions of individuals and affecting in no small measure the affairs of the world. Little boots it to say that self-consciousness in this sense is morbid, pathological, undesirable, and a product of recent pep writers and talkers. Classical writers like Carlyle, Thackeray and Hawthorne have used the term in this sense without resorting to either explanation or apology; and Archbishop Trench in his admirable essay on Calderon gives this sense a literary turn when he says of the great Spanish dramatist:

> It was not, indeed, possible for him, arriving as he did at the latter end of a mighty burst of poetry, to be other than a self-conscious poet. This burst of poetry had now lasted so long, had produced so many poetical masterpieces inviting study, had enjoyed such ample time for reflecting upon itself and upon the means by which its effects were brought about, that self-consciousness had become inevitable.[5]

A Popular Life Problem

Such precedent must be ample justification for centering attention on a topic which has

---

[5] R. C. Trench: *An Essay on the Life and Genius of Calderon*, 2nd edition 1880, p. 65.

been sorely neglected in our psychological textbooks and treatises, as if it were of no psychologist's concern. As we shall see in the next chapter, the applied psychology of self-consciousness, to judge from the number of people addicted to it, is so grave a matter that we might at least have expected some scientific treatment of the subject.

Sometimes the term "self-consciousness," even when defined as "preoccupation with one's own personality to such an extent as to suppose that one is the object of observation by others" is employed in a somewhat inappropriate sense for our practical purpose. Thus J. S. Morrill has compiled a large number of anecdotes, disclosing the boastfulness, presumptuousness and conceit of celebrities, under the title of *Self-Consciousness of Noted Persons*.

Ego-Consciousness to Refer to Undue Self-Regard

While admitting that vanity, self-esteem or self-approbation is a species of self-consciousness or emanates therefrom, it would be well

to introduce some other word for that type of
self-centredness, in order to avoid confusion.
Perhaps a term like "ego-consciousness" would
be the most suitable because the word "ego"
has always been associated in the mind of the
educated with self-regard and satisfaction with
one's self.

The Two Terms Denote Opposite Urges

The chief reason for keeping the two states
apart in nomenclature is not only that they
arise in two different instinctive urges, *viz.,*
self-aggression and submissiveness, but what is
more important, they affect the individual altogether differently. Apparently ego-consciousness, although an undesirable trait from a social or ethical point of view, is yet conducive
to achievement and self-satisfaction. It has a
positive result. Self-consciousness on the other
hand, although less reprehensible than conceit,
and sometimes even thought of as a virtue, as
we shall see later, hampers action and acts as a
depressing agency.

[39]

CHAPTER II

From the neglect of the subject of self-con-sciousness in books on psychology, one might suppose that self-consciousness in the practical sense is a comparatively rare phenomenon; and, therefore, the discussion of it should be relegated to psychiatric books, but as a matter of fact we shall see first that self-consciousness is far from being an uncommon liability, and secondly, books on psychopathology and psychi-atry, aside from a passing reference here and there in relation to a case described, ignore the subject systematically.

Dearth of Literature

It is symptomatic of the present status of the subject that even such a comprehensive volume as Taylor's *Readings in Abnormal Psychology and Mental Hygiene* has no mention of it in the very full index. Periodicals for the last ten years, whether popular or psychological, do not indicate that self-consciousness is a subject of human interest, and where an almost unique article does happen to be labelled "self-consciousness," one discovers on reading it that the text is on popularity, worry, phobia, and whatnot. Similarly, the only book which is entitled *The Psychology of Self-Consciousness,* by Julia Turner, is about on everything but self-consciousness. Truly, it might be said that psychological circles are blissfully unconscious of self-consciousness.[1] And yet, what are the facts?

A Statistical Surprise

If a thousand people of more than average intelligence were asked what, in their opinion, was their greatest personal handicap in life, more than three hundred and seventy would

---

[1] Since writing the above, a doctoral dissertation had appeared in Dutch on embarrassment (*De Verlegenheid, 1935*) in which the author, Jan Schouten, deals with a few topics taken up in this book, although from a more theoretical angle. His chapter on the expression of embarrassment in Dutch Indies is a contribution to comparative psychology and perhaps even anthropology.

[41]

answer, "Self-consciousness and lack of self-confidence." This is a fact which was revealed to the author as a result of questionnaires prepared for large University Extension classes. This result was not a little surprising at first, especially as what was true of the extension classes seemed also to hold of a class in a well-known technological institution.

The individuals making up a large university extension class range from the ages of 17 to 70 and come from many different strata of society, representing various walks of life. The students in the technological institute were youths in their late teens and early twenties.

Perhaps it may be inferred that there are more self-conscious individuals at the age of majority than at other periods in life, and that self-consciousness particularly affects the student. It would be interesting to compare the masses attending boxing and wrestling matches or baseball games with students in this respect. But even if the condition is to be found more frequently in the latter class, the large percentage of self-conscious people in our midst is well worth considering.

ORIENTATION THROUGH FACTS

Adults Do Not Appear Self-Conscious

This finding is primarily surprising because the man in the street appears to be anything but self-conscious. To judge from outward appearance, the people you meet on thoroughfares, in shops and stores, on the stock exchange, in the theatre and other public places are, if anything, too aggressive and forward, arguing and haggling, quite certain about the truth of their views and the accuracy of their statements. Is it possible that out of every thousand who jostle you on an early Saturday afternoon in the shopping district of a metropolitan city, no fewer than three hundred and seventy or 37 per cent are self-conscious and painfully aware of the fact?

All Types of People May Be Self-Conscious

The truth of the matter is that self-consciousness is a term which covers many different states of mind. Most likely even what James called the "tough-minded" will sometimes find themselves in a predicament which will make

them self-conscious, while there will be some
who will turn over in their mind again and
again the phrasing of a simple question, such
as "Have you any semi-soft collars?" to be
put to a salesman behind a counter.

Chronic and Acute Self-Consciousness

There are, indeed, even more pronounced
cases bordering on psychoneurosis, or conditions of great "nervousness", but for our present purpose, it will be sufficient to state that
there are various grades and shades of self-consciousness, and to institute a division between
the classes which I shall designate "chronic"
and "acute." The former embraces the milder
states which do not manifest themselves to the
naked eye, so to speak, of casual observers. The
acute type exposes not only the suffering individual because of the explicit behavior involved, but is called forth also by what the
"self-conscient," if such a word may here be
coined, would regard as an unusual situation,
although undoubtedly his or her mental constitution, physical condition at the time, or

some other subjective factor must have been keyed up in order that the situation might take effect. The temporal difference, that is to say, in duration, between the two types is self-understood, but not so significant as the ear-marks just alluded to. Acute self-consciousness is of a piece with emotion; chronic self-consciousness is an attitude which may at any time turn into an emotion.

We shall have to revert to the different varieties of self-consciousness according to the situations involved, when the causes and conditions of self-consciousness are under discussion.

CHAPTER III

How Does It Feel to be Self-Conscious?

The self-conscious individual may be studied from two different viewpoints: (a) from the subjective side; and (b) from the behavior angle. The subjective phase can be studied, naturally, by the subject alone. We know, for example, that in the state of self-consciousness there is a distressing emphasis of some personal quality or part of the body, the voice, the hands, posture, etc. Attention is focussed on our speech; the voice sounds as if it belonged to someone else; there are persistent images of a hazy character; also images of oneself, one's physiognomy, usually not at its best. There is a mild depersonalization, an occasional anxious mental query as to how one is appraised at a given moment by the person or persons around; there is a tendency toward self-criticism and at least a momentary implicit elevation of one's

[46]

companion or interlocutor. The greater the dependence for a favor or good grace, the more marked will the state of self-consciousness become, and the more mental tension will attend the focusing upon some feature of the self, and the more distraught and absent-minded the subject will grow. Organic complexes, constriction about the diaphragm, and sensations of strain, localized often in the fingers, sometimes thermal sensations above the knees, wobbliness, and a dazed feeling about the head are all to be considered as the mental experience of acute self-consciousness.

Objective Symptoms

Although self-consciousness is, as its name signifies, an introspective state, the behavior concomitants are nevertheless part and parcel of the whole situation. In most marked cases, the embarrassment, if not plainly visible, is at least detectable. There is a hesitation or vacillation in movement, the expression of the face changes. Blanching or blushing is frequently noticeable, and even a tremor of the hand.

[47]

Turning away of the face—in children hiding or covering their face with their hands—is one of the commonest symptoms. Bowing the head or drooping the eyes is only a variation of the concealment tendency. Blinking points to a more disturbed state. Even the tear glands may be affected by self-consciousness, and in very distressing cases, the genito-urinary organs are stimulated just as in time of unusual fright or anxiety. Curiously enough, a grin sometimes referred to as a "sheepish" grin, is often the accompaniment of self-consciousness. Giggling in adolescent girls and servants is sometimes an indication of self-consciousness.

Speech is markedly affected. Sometimes there is a stammering; at other times the individual lapses into malapropisms, that is to say, might say the "fly crows" instead of the "crow flies," becomes tongue-tied or can scarcely utter a sound. The voice, if there is no other betrayal of self-consciousness, is either unusually low-pitched or decidedly high-pitched. Gestures lose their naturalness and one's carriage or posture is strained. Perspiration is seldom

[48]

absent. Usually it is in the palms of the hand rather than in the face that the sudoriparous glands produce their secretions. The smile that a self-conscious individual sometimes succeeds in inducing in order to disguise the embarrassment is artificial, and if laughter is indulged in, it sounds hollow and smacks of the nervous hysterical variety. A peculiar awkwardness characterizes the self-conscious individual, and unless relief comes either in self-adjustment or else in the form of a tactful move by some one else, the state becomes unbearable.

Classic Description of Embarrassment

But why outline the clinical picture *in abstracto,* when we have such a classic description of self-consciousness in the vivid reminiscence of the Italian physiologist, Angelo Mosso, who tells of his first experience as a lecturer, in the opening paragraphs of his standard work on *Fear?*

> Never shall I forget that evening! From behind the curtains of a glass door I peered into the large amphithe-

[49]

atre crowded with people. It was my
first appearance as a lecturer, and
most humbly did I repent having undertaken to try my powers in the same
hall in which my most celebrated
teachers had so often spoken. All I
had to do was to communicate the results of some of my investigations into
the physiology of sleep, and yet, as the
hour drew nearer, stronger waxed
within me the fear that I should become confused, lose myself, and finally
stand gaping, speechless before my
audience. My heart beat violently;
its very strings seemed to tighten,
and my breath came and went, as
when one looks down into a yawn-
ing abyss. At last it struck eight. As
I cast a last glance at my notes, I became aware, to my horror, that the
chain of ideas was broken and the links
lost beyond recall. Experiments per-
formed a hundred times, long periods
which I had thought myself able to repeat word for word—all seemed for-
gotten, swept away as though it had
never been.

My anguish reached a climax. So

great was my perturbation that the
recollection of it is dim and shadowy.
I remember seeing the usher touch the
handle of the door, and that, as he
opened it, I seemed to feel a puff of
wind in my face; there was a singing
in my ears, and then I found myself
near a table in the midst of an oppres-
sive silence, as though, after a plunge
in a stormy sea, I had raised my head
above water and seized hold of a rock
in the centre of the vast amphitheatre.

How strange was the sound of my
first words; my voice seemed to lose itself in a great wilderness, words,
scarce fallen from my lips, to tremble
and die away. After a few sentences
jerked out almost mechanically, I per-
ceived that I had already finished the
introduction to my speech, and discovered with dismay that memory had
played me false just at that point
where I had thought myself most
sure, but there was now no turning back, and so, in great confusion,
I proceeded. The hall seemed envel-
oped in mist. Slowly the cloud began to lift, and here and there in

the crowd I could distinguish ben-
evolent, friendly faces, and on these
I fixed my gaze, as a man struggling
with the waves clings to a floating
spar. I could discern, too, the atten-
tive countenances of eager listeners,
holding a hand to their ear as though
unwilling to lose a single word, and
nodding occasionally in token of af-
firmation. And lastly, I saw myself
in this semi-circle, alone, humbled,
discouraged, dejected—like a sinner at
confession. The first greatest emotional disturbance was over; but my
throat was parched, my cheeks burned,
my breath came in gasps, my voice was
strained and trembling. The harmony
of the period was often interrupted in
the middle by a rapid inspiration, or
painfully drawn out, as the chest was
compressed to lend force to the last
words of a sentence.[1]

Although Mosso published his universally ac-
claimed book in the previous generation, it is
improbable that anyone has succeeded in draw-
ing a better picture of what goes on mentally
while one is embarrassed.

---

[1] A. Mosso: *Fear.*

Recovering from Embarrassment

Not only, however, does Mosso present the details of his disagreeable experience, but further relates the story of the recovery. The process of self-adjustment is brought about either by observable encouragement from the audience or else by a *fiat* of the will, an autosuggestion or other dynamic thought, that is to say, an idea which leads to action. Thus we read:

> But to my joy, in spite of all, the ideas began to unfold of their own accord, following each other in regular order along the magic thread to which I blindly clung without a backward glance, and which was to lead me out of the labyrinth. Even the trembling of the hands, which had made me shake the instruments and drawings I had from time to time to exhibit, ceased at last. A heaviness crept over my whole body, the muscles seemed to stiffen, and my knees shook.
>
> Towards the end I felt the blood begin to circulate again. A few minutes passed of which I remember nothing

[53]

save a great anxiety. My trembling voice had assumed the conclusive tone adopted at the close of a speech. I was perspiring, exhausted, my strength was failing; I glanced at the tiers of seats, and it seemed to me that they were slowly opening in front of me, like the jaws of a monster ready to devour me as soon as the last word should re-echo within its throat.

Mosso was describing an acute stage of self-consciousness, something which would correspond to "stage-fright," but many of us have lived through the same anguish on different occasions, even if in a lesser degree.

Oral examinations before the principal in grammar school days were torture, and not even the injunction of the teacher to take a few deep breaths were of much avail. As we look back upon that period of happy childhood, we become wroth over our own stupidity. To have taken such trifles to heart! To have spoilt not only many a day for us, but in some cases, to have deflected by such self-consciousness the whole course of our life! That is sad indeed, but alas, the wheels of time cannot be turned back.

> For of all sad words of tongue or pen
> The saddest are these: "It might have been!"

Phases of Self-Consciousness

The state of self-consciousness consists of three phases. There is first the *anticipatory* period, which may be regarded as a phobia, for then the afflicted individual is *not self-conscious so much as troubled by the thought that he or she will become self-conscious and make a display of all the unfortunate behavior concomitants.* There is the second stage in the process, which is the *actual state of self-consciousness,* occurring, as it does, upon the perception of a certain situation. It need not be preceded by the anticipatory period, but it is the typical phase in normal cases, although in the more serious pernicious affections, the worry about self-consciousness is more distressing than the very state itself. Then there is the third, or *after-phase,* which starts with the recovery from the momentary embarrassment or blushing, and is characterized by a mild feeling of disgust with oneself.

[55]

CHAPTER IV

What Happens in Self-Consciousness?

We have seen what the experience of self-consciousness is like, and how the self-conscious individual behaves in a given situation.

We may now examine the problem in the light of physiology. Just what takes place when we become self-conscious? The nervous system is, of course, beyond the ken of either the experiencing subject or the most watchful observer. The problem of self-consciousness belongs, in part, to the psychology of the higher thought processes and partly to the domain of the emotions. No experimental investigations on self-consciousness have, to the author's knowledge, been undertaken; and even if such should have been carried out to a significant degree, the results could not point to any physiological conclusions except through indirection.

A Task Requires Thousands of Nerve Operations

In a general way, however, we are justified in making certain inferences. Thus we know that whenever we are about to perform a particular task, thousands of nerves are set in operation. Thousands of paths are crossed by nerve currents. If the performer is no novice, the procedure will go on with due regard to organization. There will be no jumping or skipping, no interference, or, as it is called more technically, inhibition (except where the facilitation of one set of muscles can be brought about only by the inhibition of another set). All efforts are concentrated on the successful completion of the act begun.

Although the act has been initiated by a nerve impulse coming from the cortical part in the brain, the actual performance, i.e., the chain of processes which lead up to the result goes on automatically in the lower centers, where all habitual activities are regulated. The reason why games of skill or manual performances run off so smoothly is just that the limbs seem to move of their own accord, as if by turn. The

[57]

most difficult feat, whether in the playing of an instrument or in the hazardous walking on a tight rope, can be successfully carried out if all the part-movements which constitute the performance proceed consecutively.

Nerves Are Thrown Out of Gear

Suddenly, however, a distracting thought arises; perhaps a critic is spied, perhaps a fear crops up lest the result will be unfavorable, or perhaps the image presents itself of downright failure—and the whole orderly procedure of the nerve currents in the nervous system tends to collapse. Some of these impulses are derailed; some are telescoped or shunted. The interloper has thrown out of gear many hundreds of neurones. The thoughts about oneself, for the time being submerged, have now taken the field to themselves, and the mental organization developed for the execution of the performance is set at naught.

The Self and Work Interfere

It is somewhat strange that *self* and *work* should be so incompatible with each other. How true it is that we must put our whole self into our work, in other words, that our self (or rather the idea of the self) must not be given a chance, figuratively speaking, to float about and disturb the motor equilibrium of the nervous system.

It matters little whether the act under discussion is simple or not. The consequences are about the same, except that the more exacting task will require a longer period to recuperate. Two young ladies were listening to a violinist at a public concert. After the applause, one of them was praising the virtuoso for his poise and self-possession. Not once did he show any signs of self-consciousness.

"That is very easy," exclaimed the one, "if you know how to play. Why *should* he show any embarrassment?"

"Oh, is that so?" retorted the other, "Now you surely know how to walk. Will you just cross the hall before the beginning of the inter-mission?"

In this way a homely truth was brought home to the begrudging girl, a truth which we can verify for ourselves every time we pose for a photograph. Posing is the greatest detector of self-consciousness and even more of ego-consciousness. That is why so many photographs do not seem natural.

Self Interferes with Automatic Working of Act

Another instance which comes to mind is that of our signature. We may have the most fluent and spontaneous writing movements. Of all our writing stereotypes, the signature is the one most fixed, and as such, it certainly should not require the least care. But the moment we wish to autograph a book intended for a notable, or even to sign a letter to a person of whom we think highly, the fluency is immediately interfered with. Our hand is even more refractory when we are subscribing our name to an article in the knowledge that the signature will be reproduced in print. The thought "Now this must be especially graceful," which is incorporated in the nerve-current just passing from a group of cells in the upper part of the brain toward the group of cells on a lower level in the brain, has interfered with the automatism of the latter and, therefore, with the graphic habit which represents the signature.

We are here reminded of the oft-quoted doggerel lines which picturesquely describe the predicament of the centipede in a similar situation.

> A centipede was happy quite
> Until a frog in fun
> Said, "Pray, which leg comes after which?"
> This raised her mind to such a pitch,
> She lay distracted in the ditch,
> Considering how to run.

Fortunately, however, for the centipede, in this respect, the centipede, although it has a mind of a sort, does not think, and is, therefore, immune from self-consciousness. How some people would wish to be without the power of thought on one occasion or another!

If the thought alone were the whole of the story, the distraction would not be so telling. In all likelihood, there is a condensed mental representation of the person or persons who may view the signature, a comparison of appraisals, a feeling of insecurity about the outcome, anticipation of criticism or lack of appreciation. Our success in the matter depends upon our ability to keep these thoughts submerged until the act is completed.

The Fear Element in Self-Consciousness

If self-consciousness starts with a cortical process, it has a number of involvements lower down. In the first place, as in the case of any other emotional disturbance, the heart-beat would be accelerated, the blood-pressure in the more marked instances of "nervousness" would be heightened, and the number of red blood corpuscles increased according to the intensity of the embarrassment. Aside from these and other vascular changes, there is the gasping for breath, and redistribution of the oxygen supply, the cessation of certain gastric and intestinal processes (churning and peristaltic movements as well as secretions). The fear element in self-consciousness is to be linked up with the liberation of blood-sugar and the secretion of adrenin.

WHAT HAPPENS IN SELF-CONSCIOUSNESS

Physiological Locus

In all these processes, the sympathetic division of the automatic nervous system would be greatly affected. It is through the nerve impulses coming from the sympathetic neurones that the vaso-motor changes are brought about during the state of great embarrassment. As to which portion of the central nervous system governs that peculiar feeling of self-consciousness or "shakiness," we might set down the hypothesis that it is the *optic thalamus* at the base of the brain which is the locale of the state of self-consciousness inasmuch as there seems to have been a growing conviction, since the appearance of Bekhterev's paper in 1887, that all emotional experience is mediated through this organ. Many neurologists, including Bekhterev, Sherrington, Cannon and Head, have obtained results which point definitely to the optic thalamus as the higher centre for emotion.

Are the Glands Involved?

The question about what other glands may be activated, besides the adrenals, in the more

[63]

acute state of self-consciousness is left open. That there is a relationship between glandular balance and proneness to self-consciousness may be taken for granted, but more will have to be known both about the working of the glands and the nature of self-consciousness before any specific correlation can with justice be hazarded. Nevertheless, on the basis of a large number of empirical observations, including crucial instances, a few suggestions may be made. These, however, must be deferred to a later section.

We must consider first the nub of our whole study, *viz., What sort of individuals are given to self-consciousness,* and *what are the causes of self-consciousness?*

CHAPTER V

Before we gain access to the source of self-consciousness, it is essential that we establish with some degree of certainty just which type of individual falls a victim of self-consciousness. We shall presently see that there is not a single cause, but many causes which produce this troublesome state; true the particular effects may appear to an investigator somewhat different according to the origin, but to the individual afflicted, the baleful result is the same.

Introverts More Susceptible than Extraverts

It is well known that those who are reserved, of a retiring disposition or belong to the introverted class are more susceptible than the hale and bluff type. There seems to be a whole series of connections or links between qualities, so that the presence of the one will imply the presence of another similar quality, and the absence of another which is unlike it. Traits like sensitiveness, reclusiveness, bashfulness, diffidence, reserve, unsociability, timidity all appear to make for self-consciousness. Characteristics, on the other hand, like self-assurance, boldness, forwardness, conceit, extraversion are not usually associated with self-consciousness.

Types Against Types

With reference to types, we may range the introverted against the extraverted, the individuals who are introspective against those who are altogether unreflective, the scientist and the poet against the business man, particularly of the salesman variety, the philosopher against the politician and the actor. In the professions, the technologist and the teacher are to be ranged against the lawyer and the physician, the theologian against the evangelist or in particular the revivalist.

It will be readily seen that the latter are thrown in with people more than the former. The technologist is often a recluse, while the school teacher, because of her communion almost exclusively with children, and possibly, too, her spinster state, develops a self-depreciative attitude. Nevertheless the causes of the characteristics, I am inclined to think, are inherent rather than circumstantial, and the vocation itself is a product of the character rather than the reverse, that is to say, a salesman goes into selling because of his temperament.

The Demarcation Line Fluctuates

That a sharp line of cleavage cannot be drawn goes without saying. Even among artists of a high creative order we can find such as were scarcely known to be self-conscious, to wit, Wagner, who was, however, decidedly ego-conscious; and among actors one may find some who repeatedly recount episodes of their extreme self-consciousness, but in spite of such exceptions the tendencies do remain. Indeed, the very exceptions point to a certain contradiction in the nature of the individual. Thus Wagner was possessed of theatrical as well as of musical genius, and, therefore, enjoyed the quality, which is a part of all actors, of appropriating other personalities to himself. Such people cannot be really self-conscious when their self has assimilated the selves of others, although in spite of the collective nature of their personalities, they may stand out as distinct individualities.

Differences in Objective of Imagination

We are now in a position to understand the difference between ego-consciousness and self-consciousness, and thus come to the crux of our problem; for it must dawn upon the reader that actors, orators, statesmen, indeed, even executives, administrators and salesmen are imaginative after a fashion. Frequently, however, as in the case of the three latter, the imagination is restricted to the business in hand and does not touch upon the relation between self and others. But where the real difference comes in between the introvert and the extravert,[1] is that

---

[1] The types as well as the temperamental groups are explained in *Personality, the Crux of Social Intercourse* also in *Success in Handling Types,* both by A. A. Roback. (Sci-Art Publishers, Cambridge, Mass.)

the one keeps himself fixed and elevates the ego
of the other without comprehending him; the
other projects himself easily into the personality of others, because there is a commonness of
make-up, and thence proceeds to take the other
down a peg. The one *subjectifies his fellows;*
the other *objectifies himself.* What the introvert respects in the almost-never embarrassed extravert is his maturity and worldliness, manifested through his presence of mind.
It is like a child looking up to a grown-up person whom he regards, nevertheless, as inferior
to himself. The adult, however, whatever defects he may have, is more sure of himself, and
evinces the fruit of his *experience.* Here we
have another direction for our pursuit.

The Self-Conscious Lack Experience

The individual who is self-conscious lacks experience. Therein he resembles a child. The
nonchalant person seems to have been *born
with a certain worldliness.* He is *of* the world,
made of the same clay as millions of others,
and, therefore, instinctively knows his acquain-

tances better, and more of his environment, than does the thin-skinned sensitive deviate who, true to the laws of retarded development in human beings as compared with early maturation in animals, requires a good deal of stimulation and broadening by the exigencies of life before he can enter the hall of ordinariness.

Temperament and Self-Consciousness

What has been said about the introvert and the extravert may be applied to the temperamental categories. Of the four traditional temperaments, the sanguine is seldom given to self-conscious onsets. The true phlegmatic is too devoid of emotion to allow himself to be upset over what his audience will think of him. The choleric may at times reveal signs of embarrassment, but it must be recognized that no one with a temper can be endowed with a truly sensitive constitution. The habit of venting one's spleen already presupposes an attitude of familiarity, and familiarity is the alkaline that corrects the trait of self-consciousness. Some psychologists maintain that only the choleric, the high-strung are sensitive. Unfortunately, the word "sensitive" is not always used unequivocally. It is quite true that the choleric person will rebel against criticism and will brook no opposition, but the true test of sensitiveness is delicacy in speech and action. The choleric will not allow himself to be hurt; the sensitive person suffers in pain.

There is only one temperament-type left, *viz.*, the *melancholic*. It is from that class that the vast majority of self-conscious people are recruited. Whether they are self-conscious because they are melancholic or *vice versa* is difficult to say. Probably the particular psychophysical make-up which is responsible for the one is also at the root of the other.

The Melancholic Easily Given to Self-Consciousness

The constitutional types which yield the self-conscious battalions are undoubtedly the long-bodied (*leptosome*) and particularly the asthenic group, or fairly tall, and light (in reality ineffective) type, as well as the dysplastic (unsymmetrical in appearance), although the sources are different in each case. On the basis of the French School (*Sigaud*) the respiratory and the cerebral type are the most susceptible, and the *digestive* (in Kretschmer's scheme, the pyknic, or round, stout, thick-set type) is the least affected.

Self-Consciousness and Constitution

Of the two biotypes, the *schizothymic* and the *cyclothymic*, it is to be assumed that the former consisting of those individuals who are characterized by more or less eccentric behavior pointing to a split-off consciousness, as if there were two trains of mental experiences running parallel to each other, are prone to be timid in company. Those, on the other hand, who are elated and depressed in turn are far more at home socially.

Glandular and Other Relationships

If we can speak of glandular personalities, as Berman endeavors to do,[2] it might be surmised

---

[2] L. Berman: *The Glands Regulating Personality.*

that the self-conscious will be found mainly among the pituitary-centred people. From the point of view of activity, the hypodynamic (less energetic) individual is self-conscious. Rarely are the hyperdynamic (over-energetic) troubled with embarrassment. As to submissiveness and ascendance, the situation is less definite. Although, offhand one would take it that the more submissive a person, the more shy and self-conscious will he or she feel, we can surely recall from memory certain acquaintances who, though self-conscious in general, display an almost domineering ascendance in their attitude toward others, and, on the other hand, there are those whose submissive behavior is rather pronounced, while not exhibiting any signs of self-consciousness in society. Finally, it would be natural to suppose that self-consciousness goes hand in hand with masochistic tendencies, that is to say, the desire to receive physical pain from the sexual partner, while sadism (or urge toward administration of sexual cruelty) is a safe indication that social timidity is not one of the individual's disadvantages.

SELF-CONSCIOUSNESS SELF-TREATED

Theory Suggested Borne Out in Observation

If asked upon what evidence these conjectures are based, for they are only conjectures, it would be hard to give a satisfactory reply; since actual observations, though empirical enough, are not many; but by first of all collecting and examining these observations, then correlating the types alluded to, and making use of the process of elimination, it was possible to see that what might be expected from this collation, for example, introversion, schizoid, masochistic, leptosome, etc., is borne out in actual life. In such observations, it is the absence of negative instances to disprove one's guess which is most important.

In conclusion, let us note that the average self-conscious person inclines toward individualism in his social philosophy and mode of life rather than toward any form of socialism or communism and still less fascism.

CHAPTER VI

Self-Consciousness in Genius

Is Self-Consciousness a Lack of Confidence?

In our approach to the causes of self-consciousness, we cannot afford to content ourselves with merely an examination of the different types of average people who are tormented by this scourge, which more than any other comes from within. It has often been remarked, and is popularly believed, not without a modicum of reason, that the root of all self-consciousness is lack of confidence. We should anticipate, then, that other things being equal, the higher in the scale of achievement one mounts, the less self-conscious will one be. Nevertheless it is fully established that some of the world's greatest geniuses who surely were aware of their wonderful endowments were the most bashful of men.

SELF-CONSCIOUSNESS SELF-TREATED

A Few Outstanding Illustrations

Newton, the colossus of science who formulated the law of gravitation, Faraday, the chemist and discoverer of magneto electricity, Schubert, the great Austrian composer, Schumann, the famous German tone-poet, Tchaikovsky, the foremost Russian composer, were all extremely reserved. Shelley's life (the English poet) at Eton was made miserable because of his great sensitiveness and reclusiveness, which brought upon him the taunts of his fellow-students. Similarly, another English poet, Thomas Gray, was conscious of his effeminate appearance while a youth. One might allude to the embarrassment of the astronomer, Schubert, in society; and to the uncomfortableness of Grillparzer, the Austrian dramatist, in the company of his more aggressive contemporaries. Pestalozzi, the father of modern educational methods, presented a sorry spectacle at social functions.

Our own Nathaniel Hawthorne, perhaps the peer of American novelists, would become so panic stricken on noticing visitors approaching, that he would run out of the house to avoid meeting them. It was left for his wife to receive them as agreeably and calmly as possible under the circumstances, thus developing a poise which at first she was not possessed of.

It would take reams of paper to do justice to the mortification of famous authors as a result of this trait; for every nationality has its quota of self-conscients, particularly in the creative stratum. If we consult Samuel Smiles, the author of a notable series of inspirational books, we shall find that most people of Teutonic race are shy; and in his famous work on *Character* we read that shyness, which may be looked upon as the behavior aspect of self-consciousness is styled the "English mania," although according to him, it is characteristic of all the Northern nations.

> The ordinary Englishman, when he travels abroad carries his shyness with him. He is stiff, awkward, ungraceful, undemonstrative and apparently unsympathetic, and though he may assume a brusqueness of manner, the shyness is there and cannot be wholly concealed.

SELF-CONSCIOUSNESS SELF-TREATED

The dry, *gauche* Englishman—to use the French phrase, *L'Anglais empêtré* —is certainly a somewhat disagreeable person to meet at first. He looks as if he had swallowed a poker. He is shy himself and the cause of shyness to others. He is stiff, not because he is proud, but because he is shy; and he cannot shake it off even if he would.

Self-Consciousness, Perhaps a Gallic Characteristic

Curiously enough, in spite of Smiles's contrasting the French and the English with respect to social graces, it fell to the lot of French celebrities to shine as "self-conscients" of the first water; at least it is in French works that we find more references to that condition than anywhere else. If self-consciousness is not a Gallic characteristic (even the redoubtable Napoleon, when a youth at the military academy at Brienne, was anything but the arrogant bully he afterwards turned out to be), the habit of adverting to it frequently, at any rate, must surely be something bound up with the psychology of the French people. Perhaps the real self-conscious people are too shy to refer to it.

[78]

SELF-CONSCIOUSNESS IN GENIUS

Montesquieu's Troubles

There is the instance of the great Montesquieu, a man blessed with rank, fortune, genius, good breeding, a fine presence, worthy friends. And yet this selfsame man who had every right to be well-poised, as befitted his office as magistrate and President of the Bordeaux Parliament in France, complained bitterly of his inability to collect his thoughts when with people ... "As soon as I feel that I am being listened to," he tells us in his *Self-Portrait*, "from that moment it seems that the whole issue escapes me." In another passage, we read, "Whenever I was expected to show brilliancy in conversation, I could never do so." In the company of intellectuals, he was less subject to these spells of depression than in the company of fools, because he could lean on the understanding of the former, while he could expect nothing but ridicule from the stupid.

Rousseau, a Foolhardy Coward

The case of Jean Jacques Rousseau, whose philosophy was instrumental in bringing about the French Revolution, is even more noteworthy, for with all his vanity, egotism, and presumptuousness, this restive spirit, who more than any one else influenced subsequent European thought, was timid to the point of distraction. Toward the end of the first book of his *Confessions,* we find the following amazing utterance:

> Everything alarms and terrifies me; the very buzzing of a fly will make me shudder; I am so subdued by fear and shame that I would gladly shield myself from mortal view. When obliged to exert myself, I am ignorant what to do; when forced to speak, I am at a loss for words, and if anyone looks at me I am instantly out of countenance. If animated with my subject, I express my thoughts with ease, but in ordinary conversations I can say nothing—absolutely nothing; and the obligation to speak renders them insupportable.

It is true he was only a young lad then, perhaps no more than thirteen or fourteen, but how many boys of that age behave in the manner described by Jean Jacques a little further?

> A thousand times, both during and since my apprenticeship, have I gone out to purchase some delicacy. I approach the pastry-cook's, perceive some women at the counter, and imagine they are laughing at the little epicure. I pass a fruit-shop, see some fine pears. Their appearance tempts me; but then two or three young people are near, a man I am acquainted with is standing at the door, a girl is approaching—perhaps our own servant; I take all that pass for persons I have some knowledge of, and my near-sightedness contributes to deceive me; I am everywhere intimidated, restrained by some obstacle, my desire grows with my hesitancy; and at length, with money in my pocket, I return as I went, for want of resolution to purchase what I long for.

Maine de Biran's Lament

Maine de Biran, one of the most important French philosophers of all times, bewails his lack of progress, anxiety and self-consciousness in many pages of his *Pensées.* I shall quote only a few lines:

> If I have to pay a visit to the Court or to a person of great distinction, I become so preoccupied with the dignity of the persons I am to see, with the manner in which they will receive me that I arrive all timid and crestfallen. If I have to speak in public, I become so disturbed and uneasy about my failing memory or the weakness of my speech organs, about the glances which will be cast in my direction, that my powers are paralyzed in the very instant when I must make use of them.

The Brooding Amiel Hate His Own Defect In Another

It was because Amiel, the Swiss poet and philosopher, who but for his excessive introspectiveness and brooding, might have ranked as one of Europe's most distinguished critics, instead of being known only for his voluminous *Journal Intime*—it was because Amiel found in

Maine de Biran much of himself that he made, under date of June 17, 1857, the following entry:

> I have just followed Maine de Biran from his twenty-eighth to his forty-eighth year by means of his journal, and a crowd of thoughts have besieged me. Let me disengage those which concern myself. In this eternal self-chronicler and observer I seem to see myself reflected with all my faults, indecision, discouragement, over-dependence on sympathy, difficulty of completing a task, with my habit of watching myself feel and live, with my growing incapacity for practical action, with my aptitude for psychological study. But I have also discovered some differences which cheer and console me. This nature is, as it were, only one of the men which exist in me. It is one of my departments. It is not the whole of my territory, the whole of my inner kingdom. Intellectually, I am more objective and more constructive; my horizon is vaster; I have seen much more of men, things, countries,

peoples and books; I have a greater mass of experience — in a word, I feel that I have more culture, greater wealth, range, and freedom of mind, in spite of my wants, my limits and my weaknesses. Why does Maine de Biran make *will* the whole of man? Perhaps because he had too little will. A man esteems most highly what he himself lacks, and exaggerates what he longs to possess. Another incapable of thought, and meditation, would have made self-consciousness[1] the supreme thing. Only the totality of things has an objective value. As soon as one isolates a part from the whole, as soon as one chooses, the choice is involuntarily and instinctively dictated by subjective inclinations which obey one or other of the two opposing laws, the attraction of similars or the affinity of contraries.

Inhibitions in a Fiery Radical

Another thinker of a radical cast of mind, in

---

[1] It is to be noted that Amiel speaks here of self-consciousness as the quality of knowing well one's mental processes. In other words, as a philosopher he reverts to the philosophical sense of the term.

spite of his publicistic prowess, is Pierre Leroux, the French socialist and writer, who confesses in a letter written to George Sand, the French authoress (Madame Dudevant) that her presence overwhelms him.

> I am always too embarrassed and disturbed to say a word in your presence (which, incidentally, makes me prattle often too much.) I felt that the first time I saw you, I couldn't utter a word.

Nor was George Sand alone the cause of his embarrassment. Mme. d' Agoult, a friend of George Sand, brought about the same flustered state, so that when asked what the lady looked like (blonde or brunette, large or small) he was at a loss to say, although he had conversed with her the day before.

Chateaubriand's Ambivalent Mind

One could hardly have believed that the author of *Le Génie du Christianisme, Atala, René,* and many other universally recognized masterpieces of prose, was a prey to his own timidity, but we have Chateaubriand's own testimony for it. Despite his haughtiness, pomposity, gallantry, and boastful nature, Chateaubriand, the French writer and diplomat, was in his youth fearfully shy in the presence of women. In his *Mémoires d' outre-tombe,* he goes into considerable detail relating what a torture it had been for him to travel with a woman over night or to receive the attention of another to whom he had been presented. His presentation to Louis XVI was not so unbearable, although he tells us that he did not feel happy until he fled from the amenities of the Court at Versailles. Yet the same Chateaubriand states that when he was received a few years later by Washington he was unmoved in his presence. And he could not have been more than twenty-three at the time.

> "Neither grandeur of soul," he explains, "nor greatness of fortune or estate ever impresses me unduly. I can admire the former without being overwhelmed by it; the latter inspires me with pity rather than respect; and I never feel troubled by the gaze of any man."

[86]

SELF-CONSCIOUSNESS IN GENIUS

In Chateaubriand's tale, we sense a sort of ambivalence, or a timidity and its opposite, and while he speaks so seriously about his shyness and self-consciousness, we feel all the time that it is our sympathy to his younger self that he wishes to evoke.

We have it from his own pen that he was a shut-in personality, that he had not been able to reveal himself.

> I never talk to casual people of my interests, my plans, my work, my ideas, my attachments, my joys, my sorrows, being persuaded of the profound weariness which one causes to others by talking of one's self. Sincere and truthful though I be, I am lacking in openness of heart; my soul incessantly tends to close up; I do not tell anything wholly, and I have never allowed my complete life to transpire, except in these Memoirs. If I try to begin a story, I am suddenly terrified at the idea of its length; after four words, the sound of my voice becomes unendurable to me, and I am silent. As I believe in nothing except religion,

> I distrust everything: malevolence and disparagement are the two distinctive qualities of the French mind; derision and calumny, the certain result of a confidence.
>
> But what have I gained by my reserved nature? To become, because I was impenetrable, a fantastic something, having no relation with my real being? My very friends are mistaken in me, when they think that they are making me better known and when they adorn me with the illusions of their love for me. All the small intellects of the ante-chambers, the public offices, the newspapers, the *cafés* have assigned ambition to me, whereas I have none at all.

But his plaint does not ring so genuine as for example, Montesquieu's or Maine de Biran's. If lack of self-confidence may explain to some extent Maine de Biran's nervousness, we can only with difficulty suppose that one like Chateaubriand who was overmodest in recounting his accomplishments at every turn, who was constantly comparing himself with the greatest and who could bring himself to declaim that "With me . . . there commenced a revolution in French literature," and "What would the nineteenth century be without my writings?", that such a one could be troubled with self-depreciation.

Self-Consciousness in Particular Situations

It is by studying these great deviations from the masses, that we shall see certain qualities stand out in relief, which will thus render them more accessible to investigation. To be sure, extraordinary minds will most likely present proportionate complication. Is it not possible to entertain a superlative estimate of one's capabilities, and at the same time to lack poise and self-possession on some occasions?

Anatole France: A Terror and a Mollycoddle at Once

Perhaps a little story which Anatole France tells in his inimitable *Le livre de mon ami* (My Friend's Book) will help to throw some light on the connection between self-confidence and self-consciousness. The giant of French letters relates that at the age of seventeen he could hold his own with boys and men of every calibre. What a dashing blade he was in his ripening period! What a strong-willed fellow; how sure of himself he felt at the time. But in the company of his mother's girl friends he was completely lost. Beads of perspiration would trickle down his brow whenever he had to greet one of the young ladies, or answer a simple question, and he often reflected on the salutary advice of the misogynistic monk (Thomas à Kempis) *who in his Imitation of Christ* besought his readers to flee from women with a hasty adieu.

Anatole France's self-consciousness, then, was of a specific kind. The stimulus which touched it off was invariably the young woman, especially if she possessed the gracefulness and charm so common among flirts. There was no question of self-confidence in mental tournaments with mature minds, but the mere glance of a coquette was sufficient to throw him off his balance.

SELF-CONSCIOUSNESS IN GENIUS

Ernest Renan's Case

May we say, then, that Anatole France was not confident of himself as a gallant, as a ladies' man, even though in other respects he was conscious of his prowess? Such a conclusion is not unreasonable. There is also the case of an equally great, if not greater Frenchman, Ernest Renan, Semitic scholar, historian, philosopher and elegant essayist, who could take his place with the foremost in the world, could even address political gatherings with marked success, and who yet would become confused and muddled when holding a conversation with ordinary people. In his soul-stirring *Recollections of Childhood and Youth* (Souvenirs d'enfance et de jeunesse) we read:

> My incapacity with people of the world surpasses all imagination. I become involved, confused, embarrassed, and get lost in a tissue of blunders.

A Function of Imaginative People

Self-consciousness, I submit, is *a condition of mind peculiar to artists, and in fact all ima-*

ginative persons. Those who have never been beset by self-consciousness are of a tougher texture. Common laborers, bootblacks, hucksters, etc., are not, and probably never were, very self-conscious, (although they may, on social occasions, be aware of their menial calling in comparison, say, with a love rival.) It is a sign of mental aristocracy to ascribe to others such superior qualities as call forth a certain embarrassment in oneself. The person who has never been troubled by self-consciousness has *never lived in a sphere other than the prosaic.* Like an animal, he merely takes things for granted, and like a machine, he goes through his performances unaffected by the presence of people. Executives of the most matter-of-fact type are recruited from this class. They are efficient but their life is never deep or intense.

Shall we say then that self-consciousness is an asset which should be cultivated in spite of the well-known disadvantages to which it puts its possessor?

SELF-CONSCIOUSNESS IN GENIUS

Self-Consciousness a Temporary Necessary Stage

That is not my meaning at all. All I wish to convey is that self-consciousness is a *necessary stage* to pass through while we are immersed in our illusions. There comes, however, a time, alas, too soon, when we must give up our dreaming, when our imagination gives way to reality, when it is our turn to "do"—not necessarily others — and then we must forget the relation in which we stand to our superiors, audiences, etc., and become wholly absorbed in the purpose before us.

The moment we become deeply attached to our object and acquire an unshakable faith in our message, that moment do we lose self-consciousness. That is why preachers, evangelists, actors, statesmen, orators and others who are able to sway the masses do not display the quality of what has sometimes been called "stage-fright" to any appreciable extent, at least not after having once gone through the experience.

CHAPTER VII

STAGE FRIGHT

Agony of the Tough-Minded

The greatest bugaboo of all those who must face a public, be it ever so small, is what is known ordinarily as "stage-fright." In French, the monosyllabic word "trac", adds an uncanny flavor to the thought. .

There have been thousands of aspiring after-dinner speakers, lecturers, and clergymen who memorized their speech, address, or sermon, and after the first sentence, forgot the rest, as if their memories had become paralyzed. Some may have heard of the brave speaker, equipped with a prepared speech, who shot out his first ammunition with great aplomb. "One Hundred years ago the place where I now stand was a howling wilderness." To his complete consternation, he could not proceed after this. Somewhat of a strategist, he refused to stall, and with added momentum, he exclaimed "One Hundred years ago, the place where I now stand was a howling wilderness. Gentlemen, I repeat this for the sake of emphasis." But still his written discourse could not be recalled. For a second or two he stood tense, as if his gun missed fire, and he would have to give up, and then as if in agony he cried out "One hundred years ago to-night the place where I now stand was a howling wilderness, and I wish to God it still was, and I was in the middle of it."

The gentleman in question most likely did not belong to the self-conscious class. He may have been accustomed to deliver everything else but speeches, and the fact that he wished to make a good impression, perhaps shine among his associates with his unexpected brilliance, had blocked the nerve paths; for together with the ambition there went parallel a fear that he might lose the day and thereafter be "razzed" by his golf pals.

The almost incredible story is related by Darwin of an extremely self-conscious person, in whose honor a dinner-party was given, rising to thank his friends and going through the gestures of a studied speech while not uttering a single word, although acting as if he were speaking with marked e m p h a s i s. "His friends," Darwin was told, "perceiving how the case stood, loudly applauded the imaginary bursts of eloquence, whenever his gestures indicated a pause, and the man never discovered that he had remained the whole time completely silent. On the contrary, he afterwards remarked to my friend, with much satisfaction, that he thought he had succeeded uncommonly well."

If the Fright is Properly Timed

The "maiden speech" in Congress, Parliament or the Chamber of Deputies, because of its career-making possibilities is not only a matter of great moment to the novice in politics. It is almost a matter of life and death. There is a great deal of trepidation even with the most self-possessed, but one favorable sign is the early access of the fear. It has time with normal people to peter out, so that a state of calmness supervenes at the right moment.

Why actors should experience stage-fright is not easy to understand, although the fact is well-known. The actors as a class have enough self-confidence and *savoir-faire,* so that rarely do they become embarrassed in company. Their fear seems to come on when they first see themselves before the footlights. Many of them lose this fear after the second appearance, and not a few remember their dread even after they have become noted stars.

Illustrations from Well-Known Stars

Instead of going to the lives of the great actors and actresses of past generations we may take a little episode from a popular radio star written up by Jim Tully. The star is Jack Benny, who seems to be the most self-possessed man before the microphone. But Tully tells that he was a failure in New York. "The same sort of repartee that later was to make a radio nation laugh did not click here."

What had happened? Jack Benny or Kubelsky, as he was really called, had a bad case of stage-fright, not that he could not open his mouth or spoke in a tremulous voice, but it was evident that there was not the spontaneity which marked his sallies later. He tried in every way to gain confidence but to no avail.

The curious part of it was that in other places he was successful, in Scranton, Wilkesbarre, Altoona, Toledo, but New York, the arena of vaudeville, the metropolis, the circuit which makes or breaks was a bugaboo to him; and had it not been for another Jack, the fistic champion Dempsey, Benny might still have been a provincial comedian.

Let Tully tell the story:

"Why don't you try New York?" Jack Dempsey asked.

"I did—and flopped twice."

"Put her there," said Dempsey— "so did I It's stage fright—the people are the same there as anywhere else—I found that out—it was *me*. Go on back and lick 'em."

"I tried that too," said Jack Benny.

"But you didn't lick yourself first," returned the champion.

Benny returned to the Palace. This time he was not the same. The taut, nervous manner had gone. The second week he was moved to fourth on the bill.

"How'd you do it?" I asked.

"I kidded Brooklyn," was the answer.

From then on he was a "big timer" in vaudeville, and by "kidding" all the acts each week, he often remained in one city for a month.

Naturally the experiences of great actors and actresses, Keane, Booth, Sir Henry Irving Rachel, Sarah Bernhardt, Sonnenthal, Schildkraut, Moissi were not all of the same kind. Yet almost every one of them has related something in a like vein.

Sometimes, curiously enough, stage-fright is transferred from the stage to other places. Thus it is told of the great actor, David Garrick that once he appeared as a witness in court and became so confused and embarrassed that the judge found it necessary to excuse him.

Recently film actresses have shown similar nervousness in giving testimony.

Different Functions Produce Different Problems

Let us bear in mind also that stage-fright is not restricted to actors. There is the vocalist,

[99]

the instrumentalist, the conductor, the orator, the preacher. Each one of them has his own problems. The vocalist might know every note but might not be able to control his voice. The pianist can manipulate the piano but might forget the sequence in a concerto, or might strike a wrong note. The orator may not be able to formulate the thought in the right words, and so it goes.

A great deal may depend on what sort of an audience the performer is aware of being present. To perceive any one person of superior mastery would be sufficient to unnerve a beginner, or even an experienced artist who is inclined to take matters seriously.

It is the more or less analytic performer who is especially handicapped. The thought which occurs to such is: how can I play that part, when the creator of the rôle happens to be here just now? The performer begins to feel silly, as if a child were trying to show off, and of course the result may be disastrous. For this reason, unless there is a relationship of patronage, where the feeling of sympathy, protection or tenderness is sure to dominate the situation and create an atmosphere of encouragement, the presence of a superior artist should not be made known to the performer.

The conductor, because of his managerial function, is especially subject to embarrassment in the presence of a noted maestro. He must realize that not only may his interpretation be faulty, but his very directing, all the gestures which are involved in toning down the string instruments or eliciting volume from the brass portion of the orchestra might seem ridiculous. Directing an orchestra presupposes authority based on expertness, but how can a small town conductor wield authority in the presence of Toscanini? The question arises naturally, "Who am I to go through these antics, when a great leader may be laughing up his sleeve at my moves"?

A Solution to a Disturbing Thought

The answer to this question is simple. We cannot all be the greatest in a given field. If our ability is limited, then probably the orchestra is limited too, and the audience is not made up of notables with great expectations. In other words, we are operating in a *relative* world; and the conducting may be relatively good, notwithstanding the flaws which a discriminating critic may single out.

Very recently I had occasion to witness a choral class performance, with half a dozen of the class acting as conductors for different numbers. It was instructive to see how the more extraverted individuals gave the signal for the class to rise almost automatically, and started swaying their hands (in lieu of a baton) with no concern about either the public or their classmates. Others, again, were visibly pondering the fact that they were ordering about a class, that several of their charges might know some of the swaying to be "a boner", etc. It may be taken for granted that these reflective individuals are not of the directorial stuff. While the "so-what" attitude is baneful with the majority of the growing generation, it is just the antidote in such cases.

Above all, the greatest danger in cases of stage-fright is to dissociate oneself from the part one is playing. The moment an actor, instrumentalist or conductor feels that he is apart from the rôle, there is room for a disturbing wedge to crowd in, but the sensible thing to do is to lose one's identity and become just the actor, the pianist, the orchestra leader. There is no one then to do the reflecting or the criticizing. The movements will become spontaneous, graceful. There must be no attempt made to emulate some other performer, to start "fireworks." In the presence of celebrity, a dignified, though not stiff, restraint will never fail to hit the right mark, while an overexcited gesticulation may give evidence of a flustered mental state.

A Possible Explanation of Stage-Fright

At the opening of the chapter, the comment was made that it is not easy to see why actors who are as a class seldom embarrassed off stage should experience the feeling of stage-fright. Wittels, on a psychoanalytic basis, offers the very explanation which we are seeking, even

[103]

though the parties involved will probably not take too kindly to his solution of the problem.

In his contribution on ''Narcissism'' to the symposium *Sex in Civilization* he makes no bones about the actor's foible when he lays down the following thesis.

A lack of objectiveness, as a consequence of too high a degree of narcissism, is seen in stage fright. An actor wishes to be Hamlet, an actress, Ophelia. But they cannot rid themselves of their own Egos, which are called John Smith or Angelica Miller. They see several hundred pairs of eyes upon them, feel their narcissism endangered, and are afraid. On the other hand, it was self-amour which induced them to choose a profession in which they must exhibit themselves and perhaps force their contemporaries to admire their personalities. To this position of an exhibiting hero or heroine belongs the heroic fear, which is called stage fright behind the footlights. The old peddler, and stage fright: here we have two fully disparate conceptions. The peddler is not a narcissist, whereas stage fright belongs to a good actor, like jealousy in relation to love. It is inseparable from the vocation of acting. A good actor must be in love with himself to a certain degree. Hence it happens that in just this group we find so much overestimation of self, which sometimes borders on megalomania. An actor who does not unconsciously and secretly regard himself as a great genius is rare. Overestimation belongs to love, and he who, professionally, must be in love with himself must o v e r e s t i m a t e himself. One must greatly respect an actor, who succeeds in not exhibiting this overestimation of himself to a nauseating degree. It is impossible to play the part of kings, heroes, beauties, and to represent all the passions without becoming infected with the virus of their many personalities. As one permits the actor a free life in the sexual field, so one should grant concessions to these indispensable members of our society in the general human field also; i.e. the concession of a larger narcissism.

Every art is founded upon an augmentation of narcissism. Although in no other arts does self-amour reach such a high degree as in actors, dancers, and singers, it belongs to art everywhere, because art produces its achievements by the same mechanism as men engender their real children. The artist fertilizes himself, like a double-sexed plant, and brings a part of himself to life outside. The production is then independent of him and can survive him as the child does the parents.[1]

Whether we agree with Wittels or not, the fact that there is such a thing as stage-fright cannot be denied; and that nearly all actors and actresses have suffered at one time or another from it. Whether it is due to narcissism or not, the simple suggestions offered in this chapter to counteract its effects may be found useful, if devotedly carried out.

---

[1] Fritz Wittels: "Narcissism" in *Sex in Civilization*, p. 453.

CHAPTER VIII

Self-Consciousness as a Neurosis

Heretofore, we have dealt with what may be considered normal self-consciousness, but the consideration of the more serious cases must not be omitted.

It is not easy to draw the line between ordinary and morbid self-consciousness. A few criteria may be suggested.

Criteria of Morbid Self-Consciousness

(1) In the first place, the individual who is only normally self-conscious feels not unduly inconvenienced. He has some inner sign of a progressive improvement with age. The self-conscious neurotic does not see his way out of the morass and he experiences an urge to seek professional advice.

(2) Secondly, there is the intensity of the embarassment to be reckoned with. The discomfiture in the neurotic is painful.

(3)   Then again, there are longer anticipatory states and afterperiods in the more serious varieties, with brooding in between.

(4)   The noticeability of the onset on the part of observers is another criterion. That embraces both the extent of the indications (voice, trembling, blushing) and the frequency with which these indications occur.

(5)   The age of the individual is of some significance. Thus an access of self-consciousness at the age of adolescence is not serious, even in its intense form, whether subjective or objective, but at the age of forty, even a milder access is symptomatic of a pernicious state.

(6)   Embarrassment in the presence of some personage, whose authority or prestige would form a sort of halo, is not so much of a danger-signal as the fear of being observed by ordinary strangers.

(7)   Finally, there is the amount of interference with the regular routine of work that enters into the picture.

(8)   The most important symptom, however, of neurotic self-consciousness is the existence

of a *delusion* which is closely akin to ideas of reference.

A Sheaf of Cases

I need only consult my files for records of cases which illustrate every one of the criteria formulated.

The Case of M. O'B.

A young woman M. O'B, in the late twenties, fair in appearance but somewhat stooped and a trifle slow and awkward in her movements, with inexpressive eyes, except when she smiles, felt ill at ease because of her show of embarrassment and readiness to blush in company. In temperament she seemed phlegmatic, and when in a group of people, she gave the impression of being preoccupied. Her attitude to young men was ambivalent; apparently they did not take to her partly because of her shyness, and partly because of her mid-Victorian sentiments and tendency in dress. Yet she did not belong to the masculine, overbearing, reformer type of women, but rather assumed a matronly air.

SELF-CONSCIOUSNESS SELF-TREATED

When she consulted me for the first time, it was because she feared that her visible exhibition of self-consciousness might so annoy her employer that he would lose patience with her and engage her understudy in her place. It was not in his presence alone that she blushed, talked with a tremor in her voice and displayed other signs of nervousness. She was certain that nearly every one could read her disconcerted mind, and that when she entered the subway train she was being observed by the passengers who passed judgment on her.

When an attempt was made to make it clear to her that an efficient secretary, such as she was, would not be discharged because of her diffidence, that an intimate talk with her employer would convince her that he scarcely ever noticed her foible, and that on the contrary it would be revealed to her that her earnestness and conscientiousness were highly appreciated by him, she admitted the possibility but recoiled from the idea of broaching the matter to her superior, nor did she permit her consultant to confer with him.

SELF-CONSCIOUSNESS AS A NEUROSIS

Despite her timidity, she, in common with most self-conscious people, did not flinch from argumentation. Submissiveness was not to be linked with her shyness, although her coöperation during the treatment evinced the fact that she was not stubborn.

Asked why she should think that people sitting in the subway bothered to observe her plight, she replied plausibly enough that they would likely watch all newcomers, and that her becoming red in the face as she would take her seat would single her out as an object of study. She herself had similarly watched others come into the subway blushing, as they would settle in their seats. It is interesting to note how eager she was to project her own weakness onto others. Most likely she read signs that did not exist except in her imagination. Still there was no way out of exploding her fiction, except by actual experimentation. Soon after her consultation an incident occurred which could be regarded as a test case.

SELF-CONSCIOUSNESS SELF-TREATED

Delusion in Regard to Others' Observation of Oneself

On one of her consultation visits, she stated that her condition had much improved since beginning treatment, but that her being watched closely in class during a lecture was disturbing to her, and she suffered, in consequence, a relapse for a day or two. As her consultant was not aware of her enrolling as a student in his class, and as she sat at the further end of the rather long hall, and as he was not in the habit of looking into the audience while speaking, the remark was a distinct shock. What further proof then was needed than this mistaken idea to demonstrate that the young woman was deluded about other observers too? This revelation served to enlighten her greatly and, in conjunction with various practical suggestions which she more or less followed, caused her to change her attitude toward people as well as her point of view with regard to self-consciousness.

In the case just described, there did not seem to be any other complications involved aside from self-consciousness. The fear of losing her job in a period of depression is after all not far out of the way when positions are few and far between. The delusion is about the only serious component of the whole state.

Case of R. B. Exaggerating Others' Brilliancy

At times, however, the feeling of self-consciousness grows into a regular ailment to the extent even of lowering bodily tonus and impairing health, as may be seen from the extract of a letter written by a young married woman R. B., who was seemingly oppressed by the size of her inferiority complex. She was a comely matron with a good deal of what is ordinarily referred to as personality. From appearance sanguine and yet in reality, according to her own testimony, melancholic, she lost confidence in herself after moving in the society of her husband's friends, whose cleverness she exaggerated and whose bravado she mistook for brilliancy. Being of a serious and naïve turn of mind, she would be apt to take in good faith all the yarns and Munchausen stories which were related in her presence for her mystification, a form of banter common to the smart Aleck and "wise guy" type of salesman. As she made no effort to dispute the stories or to expose their absurdity, her puzzled look would be greeted with a guffaw, whereupon she would hang her head in shame. But let her speak for herself.

In my own crowd of boys and girls, I always used to lead; nothing was decided upon without me and I felt equal to any of them. When I met all these folks in my husband's crowd, I began to feel that they would think I was young and foolish, and I used to feel that they would criticize him and say "Oh! What a girl he picked." This kept working on me, and that is my complex now. I feel inferior because I feel I am not as clever as the next one. This feeling has been growing over a period of three years, and it has become so strong I am afraid to give my opinion on things for fear of being laughed at or made fun of. I have tried to laugh myself out of it, reason

it out, etc., but it gets the best of me.
With this complex it seems I have become terribly self-conscious. I think
I have always been more or less self-
conscious but not like I am now. Just
a short time ago, my husband was
going to New York on business and he
took me along. We went over the road
and with us were an uncle and aunt of
mine, a fellow named Frank (I name
him because it will be easier to refer
to him), his sweetheart, my husband
and myself. I was miserable during
the trip. If I have an inferiority complex, this boy Frank has a superiority
complex, and I was so terribly self-
conscious in his presence that I
couldn't eat and enjoy my food. He
has such a superior air, and if I could
assume a like attitude everything
would be all right but the trouble is
that I cannot. Sometimes people say
things to me, and for the moment I
cannot answer so well or so quickly
and that makes me feel that way too.
I had the feeling that this fellow was
talking about me or laughing at me.
I was at ease with my aunt and uncle.

It seems that this time, however, was the worst of all. After eating I became so nauseous and would throw up the biggest part of what I had eaten. It seems that just the sight of this fellow would make me get that self-conscious feeling and as soon as I felt that way I couldn't hold my food.

I realized that the thing for me to do is not to think of myself and put my mind on other things. In order to do this I have joined several charitable organizations in the city, have been elected to two executive boards, walk, take drives with some of my friends and still this thing persists. It is as if I were two people; one doing all these things and yet the other looking on and never rid of that self-conscious feeling.

During that trip to New York, I could hardly sleep at all at night. My dreams or thoughts were all about these things.

I have talked to myself and tried to reason it out, also if I should see this fellow that upsets me so, I have tried to feel strong enough not to care about all this and not to be self-conscious. Yet when I think I am strong, then that feeling comes over me and it is so strong that it excludes every other thing from my mind.

My head throbs and aches and I have gone to bed many a night with the wish that I never see the morning sun again.

The Unconscious and Organic Disturbance

It is quite evident that there is a condition of hysteria here which points to a psychoanalytic source. The presence of Frank, and what is worse, his *fiancée,* in this tale is not to be considered as insignificant. There is a strong indication that this young woman cared more for Frank than she would be willing to admit even to herself. Her very vomiting in consequence of this incident is symptomatic, but it was impossible to discover all the cross-currents and under-currents by correspondence or by infrequent interviews.

SELF-CONSCIOUSNESS SELF-TREATED

A Case of Self-Consciousness With Disastrous Conflicts

A combination of phobia and self-consciousness is exemplified in the case of a homosexual woman, who is apparently a person of education and refinement and yet gives evidence of possessing the stigmata of degeneration. From her remarkably detailed and revealing document, let me, meanwhile, select only that portion which bears on her stage-fright, which is the consequence of a relationship that is out of kilter with her environment. There is every likelihood that her condition has been aggravated by her inner conflict rather than by the domineering attitude of her former accompanist. Her disintegrated personality speaks out in the following *De Profundis* passage:

> When about to play in public, at first
> I fear I shall forget certain notes but
> find that even when I play with notes
> I am still fearful. If I succeed in dis-
> pelling thoughts of failure prior to
> playing, I am seized with fear while
> performing, becoming so tense, that I

am rarely able to get there. I suffer the preceding nights head-strain, and have dreams of failure, of breaking the bow, of failure to give out the sound and of forgetting. There is a decided relief to awake in the morning to reality. Have now given up playing; cannot play acceptably and the strain is too great. There seem two sides to me—the one, able to play and desiring to, another, fearful and incompetent. To experience the sensation of feeling unable to play is, I imagine, to feel the sensation of hanging to a limb over a precipice and feeling the hands no longer able to hang on—powerless.

At the time of my breakdown a few years ago, I was playing with an overly aggressive accompanist who insisted on my playing half-prepared numbers of too great difficulty.

Other Disastrous Cases of Self-Consciousness

Case after case could be cited. One patient never enters a store, particularly a department store, without feeling that he is about to be accused of theft. Another, a woman who has already made one unsuccessful attempt to end her life, is so conscious of herself and of the gap between her and the world that she cannot make friends anywhere, has no faith in people and as she talks, she twists her head in such a manner that by no chance can her interlocutor catch a glimpse of her face.

Self-Consciousness May Border on Paranoia

To go into the possible explanation of each case would take us too far afield. In most of the severe instances of self-consciousness, there is a more or less extensive involvement, so that the state of self-consciousness is only a symptomatic link in a large chain of neurosis and possibly degeneration (by degeneration is meant the progressive impairment of the nerve tissue). Self-consciousness in its extreme forms may border on paranoia. Persons harboring ideas of self-reference begin with the belief that they are under surveillance, and end with the conviction that there is a conspiracy against them. In benign self-consciousness, the tendency is merely recognized as a subjective state, accentuated by concomitant awkwardness. It is when the self-conscious individual's insight is distorted and the subjective condition is attributed to the bystander's conduct, that the danger-line is sighted.

People who exhibit this unfortunate mark are schizoid or schizophrenic, or mentally dissociated, that is, if we are to use figurative language, a number of ideas have broken away from the mainland and are floating aimlessly about in the sea of the mind. Having no moorings, sometimes separate ideas are attached to *this* archipelago, at another time to a different one. The loose mental elements will sometimes collide, sometimes adhere to one another, but to restore them to their original places in the mental economy is a good deal more difficult than to cause the two beads in the well-known puzzle to take their place in the respective depressions under the glass top.

If we cannot enter into the discussion of the causes and conditions of the grave cases of self-consciousness, because of the entanglements with psychiatry and psychoanalysis and be-cause *self-consciousness in such instances is a symptom rather than an independent disturb-ance,* we can at least take up the causes of self-consciousness in general.

CHAPTER IX

What Are the Causes of Self-Consciousness?

A. Permanent and Temporary Conditions

Here and there we have already touched upon the causes and conditions of self-consciousness, but now we must come to grips with the core of our whole inquiry.

Before we go any further, let us not delude ourselves by seeking the one cause, as if there could not be many. To be sure, self-consciousness may manifest itself in different variations because of the plurality of causes; but we have not advanced so far as to be able to study all the particulars of the gradations. It may be old-fashioned in our twentieth century to make an allusion to the Aristotelian conception of causes. But it is better to transgress against the call of modernity than against the demands of clarity.

SELF-CONSCIOUSNESS SELF-TREATED

Separation of Sets of Causes

There are psychologists belonging to a certain school who, when dealing with causes, make it a practice of lumping all the causes they can think of, regardless of their *mediacy* or *immediacy,* directness or indirectness, superficiality or fundamentality, and endogenous, that is to say, growing out of one's own nature, or environmental character. For methodological purposes, it will be necessary to examine these different sets separately. When we ask ourselves what it is that people are self-conscious *about,* we are in a way answering the question: What makes them self-conscious? Yet even a tyro can see that we have not begun to probe the deeper problem. For a beginning, it is no doubt well to consider briefly the efficient causes, that is to say, the events or acts which immediately bring about the state. They may help to give us an insight into the underlying causes, and perhaps, too, the motives; for the unconscious motives of the individual are of paramount importance.

CAUSES OF SELF-CONSCIOUSNESS

Individual and Group Differences

In listing the objects which occasion the mental condition under discussion, we are not in a position as yet to arrange them in any order according to extensity or intensity. Aside from individual differences, there are sex differences and racial differences. A woman will feel self-conscious about her looks more often than a man. An Englishman and a Frenchman will not be affected by the same stimuli. Much again will depend on the environment, vocation, age of the individual and probably other circumstances. Sometimes there are compensatory factors which make the approach less accessible to observation.

Stratification of the Various Causes

Perhaps it will be of some use to sketch the relationship of the various causes in the form of a rough diagram. The type of vase which spreads out gradually toward the top may serve to represent the stratification of the various causes. The hereditary (constitutional) equipment, which provides the dynamic key-note to the whole system, will be sought in the narrow neck or, if the metaphor is more appropriate, leg of the vessel. Then, on top, spread out but more shallow are the fixed circumstantial reasons (appearance, physique, intelligence), then still higher up, and more spread out, are the momentary environmental causes, or the actual occasions, including sexual, racial, occupational, local, (that is, where one happens to be at a certain time) and other factors.

These various sets of causes activate each other reciprocally, and in either direction—the heredo-constitutional ones generating the *élan,* or urge, while the environmental ones supply the occasion. Of course this division is more or less relative, for what is permanent today may become temporary tomorrow, and *vice versa.*

Pupils at school may be self-conscious because of their surname, if it happens to be either an unusual one or indicative of a racial affiliation. Miss Cohen, when she is called upon to recite, may be as embarrassed in an Irish community as Miss O'Sullivan in a Jewish community, but outside of the school environment, the name, except perhaps that most people would prefer more individual distinguishing marks, does not bother the self-conscious person.

Circumstantial Causes

In general we may say that a normal individual is self-conscious about his physical defects, intellectual insufficiency or volitional deficiency. Moral delinquency is also a circumstantial determinant of self-consciousness, although paradoxically enough, one would have to be moral to begin with, in order to be weighed down by this failing.

Masturbation in youths between the ages of 15-21 is a common cause. Even though they may be enlightened as to the harmlessness of this habit, they cannot help feeling that something is amiss. A young Italian who confessed that his self-consciousness was largely due to this practice, when asked why he did not follow the example of his pals, replied that he wished to save the money. Here then is an added feature: parsimony. He feels different from others, which makes him feel guilty. That makes him self-conscious particularly in the presence of the opposite sex, this bringing on bashfulness and gawkiness. This in its turn affects the attitude of young women toward him and so we are in the midst of a vicious circle.

More commonly, it would seem, people are embarrassed about their social status, humble birth, lack of money, poor clothes, domestic dissatisfaction or discord, unprepossessing relatives, race, and last but not least, certain psychoneurotic twists, which can hardly be classified with any of the other categories.

A Physical Defect As Cause of Self-Consciousness

Now to be aware of a physical defect, whether a wart on the face, a raucous voice, or halitosis, and to behave in a self-conscious manner on account of it are not inseparable facts. The one does not fully account for the other, because there are so many who do not allow themselves to be disturbed over their flaw, while some are beside themselves with chagrin.

Vauvenargues, Self-Conscious About Appearance

Vauvenargues, the young French philosopher and moralist, who was incontestably one of the most sagacious men of his time, confessed, in a letter to Mirabeau, the famous French statesman, that he wished he had a more impressive appearance. Vauvenargues' comparative awkwardness stood in the way of his taking his proper place in the army; and probably his shyness was due partly to his introspective nature, and partly to his plain features and expression. He would often lapse into fantasies about his subtlety, grandeur and majesty according to the particular sublime idea which would occupy his mind, and associate this or that quality with his physiognomy, but one glimpse into the mirror would be sufficient to crush him. He would be as much surprised as if he were to look at a Cyclops or to see a Tartar.

If Vauvenargues entered into his own shell because of his poor appearance, which most likely inhibited him in carrying on an animated conversation, Stendhal, who was at one time rated as the greatest psychological novelist in Europe, was anxious about his wearing apparel and lack of funds.

Environmental Stimulus

We may notice in most cases of self-consciousness, the larger (socially) *environmental,* and not merely the *circumstantial* factor. In Rome you are expected to be like the Romans, but what, if you cannot? It is very well known how ill at ease some of the *parvenus* appear to be at social functions, how wishing to keep up with the Joneses sometimes leads to a nervous tension which ends in a collapse. The demands of the "smart set" are too much for certain temperaments, yet where one moves in certain society, perhaps for business reasons, the code has to be followed. Frequently, either one or the other of a married couple suffers considerably because he or she does not "fit in." In another society, there would be little occasion for self-consciousness. Thus it is in many instances a relative matter.

An unkempt man will not mind so much being seen by an old scrub woman, but will demonstrate his discomfiture in the presence of a pretty and well-dressed young woman. In this case, his ungroomed condition is the efficient or acknowledged cause; the sex instinct, in conjunction with the interplay between assertion and self-abasement, the deeper-lying cause.

Three Interacting Causes

Every normal situation which arouses the self-conscious state may be divided into these three categories. We may talk of three layers of causes, the deepest being in the unconscious realm, the middle one represented by the condition of which the individual is conscious, and the most superficial or immediate cause being the momentary perception of the object which precipitates the reaction. The term "reason" may be applied to the cause of the middle layer, because it is the one which is acknowledged, if only to himself, by the individual involved. If asked, "Why do you feel disconcerted in company?" the *reason* will be given as a certain physical or mental condition (hare-lip, stuttering, etc.).

Other Physical Handicaps

The physical conditions embrace not only such things as voice or speech defect, gait, gesture, figure, complexion, malformations, posture, moles, uncouth appearance but even conditions of health. Anemic people, those suffering from asthma or hernia are more likely to show embarrassment than perfect specimens of health. Awkwardness also belongs among the physical causes. In fact, it is usually felt more keenly than other defects, and conversely a graceful person is less liable to be troubled by self-consciousness. Apparently the *free and natural control of the voluntary muscles puts one at ease in spite of certain visible flaws.* This is a point to be borne in mind with regard to prevention and treatment.

Intellectual Insufficiency

As to conditions in the intellectual sphere which bring on self-consciousness, they vary from downright stupidity to remarkable intellect, but the latter lacking in brilliance and *esprit.* There exists many a sot who is not upset about his mental deficiency and there is more than one college professor who feels downcast because he cannot engage in *salon* conversation, turn a felicitous phrase, or come back with a striking repartee.

Again, the pressure of the environment, circle or set, as well as the goal idea of the individual, is to be taken into consideration. Oliver Goldsmith would become self-conscious (or perhaps better ego-conscious) if anybody else was praised or treated with deference in his presence. There are many others who would like to shine in almost every sphere of endeavor, while the majority are satisfied with but one field of action.

The Self-Conscious Equation

It is when ambition is relatively high and achievement low that self-consciousness makes itself felt through the medium of what is ordinarily called *lack of self-confidence*. Of all the circumstantial causes, this seems to be the one most professed and most frequently referred to, and is closely allied with the inferiority complex, as used by the layman. The formula we should suggest then is

$$\frac{Ambition}{Achievement} = \text{Self-Consciousness},$$

showing that inasmuch as achievement fails to measure up to ambition, self-consciousness increases.

Self-Confidence May Be Lack of Will, and Poor Emotional Tone

Lack of self-confidence is not in reality an inner confession of intellectual insufficiency. Quite often it is a self-reproach at not having been able to accomplish something worth while with the brains at one's disposal. It harks back to the *will* at least as much as to the intelligence. Perhaps for this very reason, it is so weighty; and in not a few cases, the affective (dealing with the feelings, emotions, sentiments, etc.) system is also below par. People who underestimate their own ability are as a rule apathetic, carry an air of torpor, and because there is wanting in them the emotionally colored impulse, they lack initiative, and justify their indifference or indolence by repeatedly telling themselves and others that their self-assurance is at an ebb. Yet, in disagreements or differences with friends, then can work up an astonishingly violent temper, which is a clear indication that their psychic energy is not rationally directed.

Self-Consciousness Indicates a Lack of Credit

People who speak about their lack of self-confidence do not intend to give the impression that they lack ability, but rather that they do not give themselves enough credit, that they fear they are not equal to the task; and it is the knowledge that this fear is a permanent obstacle in the way of success, thwarting all their ambitions, which makes them such a prey to self-consciousness. But why should these individuals lack self-confidence in the first place, and why, possessed of this negative quality, should they take it more to heart than others? It becomes clear that lack of self-confidence is not a fundamental, but rather an environmental cause. The deeper-lying causes and conditions of self-consciousness will have to be sought in the constitutional make-up of the individual, and probably also in certain dynamic factors which are, so to speak, hidden from view and must needs be unfolded in the light of modern personality theories.

B. Hereditary Causes of Self-Consciousness

It has become fashionable of late to discount the influence of heredity in shaping our traits; and a number of schools in psychology have joined hands with the mechanistic and behavioristic groups to belittle the results of researches in genetics and to proclaim the potency of exclusively environmental factors.

Behaviorist Denies Self-Consciousness Is Innate

The behaviorist will deny outright that self-consciousness has an innate basis, and will maintain that the individual so affected has had a faulty conditioning, a poor upbringing. According to the logic of the behaviorist, the infant would be expected to show self-consciousness at birth in order to establish the claim that self-consciousness is largely the product of an inborn disposition. The appeal to the layman of such a reassuring view is obvious. A behaviorist ought to be able to exorcise the evil spirit of self-consciousness almost in the twinkling of an eye. The hocus-pocus consists in reconditioning the patient. The amount of reconditioning necessary would depend on the strength of the original conditioning.

Conditioning

Although I had referred to conditioning as a cause in my *Self-Consciousness and Its Treatment,* a captious critic reviewing the book in a technical journal spoke of my neglecting to mention this keynote of the glib "fixers."

The conditioned reflex which was brought into vogue by the late Ivan Pavlov needs no exposition for the millionth time. Who has not read hundreds of times about the salivation of the Russian dogs when a dinner bell was sounded?

But let it be remembered that we are dealing with human beings, not with dogs, and more-

over, not with a sensory experience, but with a
fundamental state in which the injection of the
self is involved. We can readily understand
that an individual can be conditioned to fear,
love or hate something which he had seen,
heard, or smelt at the time he had undergone a
definite emotional experience. We all know
that anything which reminds us of happier
days will cheer us, and *vice versa,* everything
associated with a state of distress will tend to
revive that original state. But can we apply
this same mechanism to self-consciousness?
Shall we say that at some time or another in
childhood, an incident occurred which made us
feel ashamed, that a tactless teacher or
thoughtless parent had brought down our self-
regard, and thus we had became self-conscious
ever since? It strikes me that this is putting
the cart before the horse; for only sensitive
children will react thus to a scolding or abuse.
Hence the particular trait or disposition must
have been there in the first place. Even if it
should be retorted that constant ridicule would
bring on self-consciousness, examples may be

adduced of individuals who did not succumb to such exposures in spite of the harshest treatment while children, and on the other hand, it may be easily seen from observation, that at a very tender age, one child may be self-conscious and another not show this tendency. That raillery and ridicule, poor circumstances, humble surroundings, etc., aggravate the original trait in most cases cannot be denied, and so much of the conditioning theory may be taken for granted, but to make conditions in the childhood of the individual responsible for every subsequent manifestation of self-consciousness is assuming what is yet to be proven.

Reconditioning, from our own standpoint, is nothing more than making the individual see the light through conferences. Enlightening the person affected changes his point of view, makes him see things in a new perspective; and thus his attitude toward people takes on a different mode. This form of treatment does not necessarily refer back to childhood experiences, but deals primarily with the present problems and situations of the individual, the past history furnishing merely a background.

Adler Is An Environmentalist

Adler's individual psychology is an unfriendly ally to behaviorism in this regard, for according to his doctrine, we are to understand that the child's early treatment on the part of the parents, brothers or sisters would explain the whole matter. Again there is a *Pollyanna* touch in this easygoing method. There was a time when self-consciousness could be best accounted for by bodily organ inferiority, which is reasonable enough, but of course this mode of approach does not provide so easily for a speedy cure, as would the environmental view.

The psychoanalysis of Freud too would, on general principles, trace the trouble to early experiences in the life of the afflicted individual, which, when repressed in the unconscious, would brew the concoction known as self-consciousness; but as we are coming to the consideration of these dynamic factors in the next chapter, we need not be detained here with the position of the opponents.

CAUSES OF SELF-CONSCIOUSNESS

Self-Consciousness Indicates Self-Assertion Instinct Is Weak

It is the author's opinion that the self-conscious person is born with a weak instinct of self-assertion, or a strong instinct of self-abasement (McDougall), in either case bringing on as a necessary sequel compensatory reactions. What the organic or constitutional substratum of this biological fact may be is for the present not known, although in the discussion of the sort of people that are self-conscious, we have had a few possible clues.

A Fault Which Runs in Families

Whenever a self-conscious patient comes to me for consultation, I make it a point to inquire about the antecedents and members of the immediate family with regard to the trait in question. Invariably it is found that self-consciousness "runs in the family," and that for the most part, in accordance with the principles of cross inheritance, the daughter takes after the father and the son resembles the mother in this respect. It is too much to suppose that in these parallels, there have been present exactly the same conditions in education, upbringing or treatment by the *milieu*.

Notwithstanding the claims of the environmentalists, there is still an abundance of evidence that points to the hereditary causes of timidity in all its forms, which would include the disposition of self-consciousness and phobias; and one may cite an array of authorities that subscribe to the endogenous view: Hartenberg,[1] for example, among the older writers, McDougall,[2] and, more reservedly, Kahn,[3] among recent writers.

---

[1] P. Hartenberg: *Les Timides et la timidité.*

[2] Wm. McDougall: *Social Psychology* and *An Outline of Abnormal Psychology.*

[3] E. Kahn: *Psychopathic Personalities.*

CHAPTER X

DYNAMIC THEORIES OF SELF-CONSCIOUSNESS

Dynamic Psychology Draws On Inference

We have surveyed the causes and conditions of self-consciousness and have found there were three levels. We now have more or less of an idea as to what induces self-consciousness, bashfulness or embarrassment, but the *modus operandi* of the deeper-lying causes is still beyond us; and for obvious reasons. Where the facts end, theory begins.

Dynamic psychology differs from the older introspective science of Wundt and his disciples in that it lays stress on inference and fills in the gaps by theoretical entities which are assumed to operate in a region that is not accessible to consciousness.

The question: Why are some people prone to be self-conscious as compared with others? will be answered variously by representatives of different schools. Let us review some of the main theories, starting from the constitutional and organic standpoint.

Question of Organic Weakness

Certainly it would be a desideratum to be able to say definitely what is the organic basis of the disturbance. There is a possibility that the individual who easily becomes embarrassed and is in constant fear of this occurrence lacks the normal supply of nervous energy. We do notice that self-consciousness is to be found more in the weak-minded than in the opposite categories. Considering, however, that self-consciousness reduces with age, we should be constrained on the above view to gather that as the individual grows older, his nervous energy increases, which does not seem to be in accord with the facts. That nervous insufficiency may be a contributing cause, one of many factors, we may well believe, but the evidence does not warrant making it the *fons et origo* of self-con-sciousness.

Dysfunctioning of Endocrine Glands, Little Known

Is there perhaps a hormone then which because of its injection in the blood-stream produces this unwelcome state? But we know comparatively so little about the hormones that any hypothesis put forward in this direction could be accepted only as a rough guess. We may be in a position to study the problem empirically after we have perfected the methods by which the index of secretion or *index incretorius,* as it is called technically, could be determined in every given individual. One could then test a self-conscious person for an excess of this or that secretion. In a previous section, it has been suggested that self-consciousness probably has something to do with the pituitary function. The thymo-centred individual gains our attention next because the thymus gland is fully developed only in childhood and self-consciousness for the most part peters out after the age of adolescence, but then again the parallelism is not at all convincing.

SELF-CONSCIOUSNESS SELF-TREATED

Chemistry of Self-Consciousness

That self-consciousness and introspective-ness are to some extent dependent on chemical alterations in the organism may be concluded from the fact that partaking of liquor will tend to reduce the intensity of either of the states mentioned. We may recall the story of how Martin Luther, the great reformer, when Professor of Theology at Wittenberg advised an overscrupulous and self-conscious student to go on a spree, in order to overcome his scrupulosity and brooding.

For all that, even if it is established that the ingestion of drugs or liquor affects our state of mind, as it does in most emotions, there is still no proof forthcoming that the influence is direct. In other words, the cause of the reduced self-consciousness on the administration of a drug may be the *banishing of the idea or images* directly responsible for the self-conscious state and the reinstatement of a different set of ideas to take their place. The organic cause then becomes incidental and not specific, which, if it were a direct cause, it would necessarily have to be.

THEORIES OF SELF-CONSCIOUSNESS

Self-Consciousness a Functional Trouble

We are safer, therefore, in the assumption that self-consciousness is a functional affair deriving its impulse from the instincts. According to McDougall all bashfulness hinges upon the self-regarding sentiment and is directly brought about by the struggle between the two opposed instincts of "self-display and self-abasement, with their emotions of positive and negative self-feeling." . . .

> Our negative self-feeling is evoked by the presence of persons whom we regard as our superiors, or who, by reason of their number and of their forming a collective whole, are able to make on us an impression of power; but it is not until our positive self-feeling is also excited, until we feel ourselves called upon to make a display of ourselves or our powers, to address the audience, to play a part as an equal among the superior beings, or even merely to walk across the room before the eyes of a crowd, that we experience the slightly painful, slightly

pleasurable, but often very intense, emotional agitation which is properly called bashfulness. Whether this state is at all possible in the absence of self-consciousness it is difficult to say. For although either instinct may be excited quite independently of, and prior to the rise of, self-consciousness, it would seem that the idea of the self and some development of the self-regarding sentiment are necessary conditions of the conjunction of the two opposed emotions; in their absence one of the opposed emotions would simply preclude or drive out the other. In situations that evoke bashfulness the negative self-feeling is, perhaps, as a rule, more directly induced by the presence of the other person or persons, while the positive self-feeling is more dependent on the idea of the self and on the egoistic sentiment.[1]

Self-Consciousness Indicates Self-Assertion as Well as Self-Abasement

In his *Outline of Abnormal Psychology*, McDougall no longer speaks of a struggle between

---

[1] Wm. McDougall: *An Introduction to Social Psychology,* (12th edition) pp. 146-147.

two opposing impulses but of a *"compound or
blend of the opposed affects of self-assertion
and submission"* as the dynamic *quale* of embarrassment. In the self-possessed individual,
there is a normal oscillation, striking a mean,
between the instinct of self-assertion and self-
abasement, while in the self-conscious person,
the pendulum swings too much in one direction,
with a resulting back-bounce. The easily embarrassed person is not exactly submissive. He
or she may be self-assertive, opinionative and
proud, as most sensitive and self-conscious
people are. It is only in this way that we can
understand the touchiness of the self-conscious.
They are embarrassed because they take themselves too seriously, because they expect too
much of themselves and because they are too
earnestly interested in the impression they
make. Their "ego" is sublime, it must not lose
one tittle of its dignity and grandeur. And yet
every new occasion offers a challenge whereby
the "beloved ego" is in danger of being taken
down a peg.

All this is, to be sure, not argued inwardly,

but there is a mental set which is its equivalent; and this mental set predisposes the individual both to sense the approach of ridicule and to feel hurt about it.

Self-Consciousness as a Compensatory Fantasy

There is a theory which has been advanced in psychoanalytic quarters to the effect that the self-conscious individual is endeavoring by way of compensation to draw attention to his or her person, because of the original unimpressiveness or external insignificance which is usually the characteristic of self-conscious people. The analogue of this phenomenon would, of course, be the old maid's delusion whereby an old and ugly-looking spinster might accuse men of wishing to force their attentions on her. In the self-conscious person, the operation presumably takes place on a lower level or rather unconsciously, since the projection is not so manifest as in the old maid's case, seeing that we must resort to surmise. There is no doubt a resemblance between the two in that the ''self-conscient'' of the less normal variety supposes that he or she is being observed and judged upon by others where there is no foundation for it, just as the spinster imagines that she is the object of men's ardent desires. In this way a *motive* is, for the first time, established for self-consciousness, namely, to enjoy in fantasy what one is denied in reality; for as James has put it so masterly in his classical chapter on the Self:

> No more fiendish punishment could be devised, were such a thing physically possible, than that one should be turned loose in society and remain absolutely unnoticed by all the members thereof. If no one turned round when we entered, answered when we spoke, or minded what we did, but if every person we met "cut us dead," and acted as if we were non-existing things, a kind of rage and impotent desire would ere long well up in us, from which the cruelest bodily tortures would be a relief; for these would make us feel that, however bad might be our plight, we had not sunk to such a depth as to be unworthy of attention at all.

[151]

It is difficult to evaluate this theory, although it is plausible enough, because "self-conscients" do not admit that they are attention-starved, but rather assert that they prefer to be left alone; and this seems to be true of the average self-conscious individual. In the more pernicious and perplexing cases, however, there is some ground for the "wish" hypothesis.

Inferiority Feeling

This brings us close to the inferiority feeling theory which has been popularized so much by the Viennese psychiatrist, Alfred Adler. The dynamic aspect of his individual psychology is a bit hazy because, in the first place, Adler makes very little of the unconscious in his system and elevates the complex, which is always an unconscious entity, into a feeling, which is necessarily an element of consciousness. It is when he speaks of "neurotic arrangements," "fictive goal" and "masculine protests" that the dynamic symbolism is introduced.

Inasmuch, however, as the inferiority feeling has been associated with the self-conscious tendency by so many of the younger set, it would behoove us to make more than passing mention of Adler's view in this connection.

Adler Slights Subject of Self-Consciousness

Perhaps it is because the connection seems so patent that little is made of self-consciousness as such in Adler's works; or, in part, the circumstance may be due to the fact that this state is considered too trivial and inconsequential to dwell on alongside of the description and analysis of genuine neuroses. It must be said, nevertheless, that self-consciousness enters as a constituent of some of the neuroses at least, just as hallucination is generally a component of the psychotic syndrome (combination of symptoms constituting a mental derangement).

Self-Consciousness, Sign of Inadequate Compensation

If then we take it that every inferiority feeling is grounded in some organic defect or taint, as Adler would have us believe, then self-consciousness will be due to the inadequate com-

[153]

pensation of the individual in his effort to rise
above the consequences of this personality flaw
which, as time goes on, brings him into conflict
with the environment (parental, fraternal, social, domestic). We must gather, then, that he
who has conquered his self-consciousness has
achieved a high level of compensation.[2]

Guilt Complex

Another theory, calculated to account for the
graver conditions of self-consciousness, which
are invariably attended by blushing, with the
consequence that the sufferers develop *ereuthophobia,* or dread of blushing, implies that the
''self-conscient'' is beset by qualms of conscience, which he or she has in vain sought to
repress. Stekel is prepared to saddle these un-
fortunates with all sorts of paraphilias, or sex

---

[2] In some of Adler's books there is a hint that self-conscious
people use their handicap as an excuse for their lack of initiative; in other words, they seem to say "What would I have
not achieved, if it were not for my self-consciousness?" Adler
does not employ the word, but the attitude he discusses may
well be one born of self-consciousness, although naturally he
uses the term "inferiority complex." See especially his *Science
of Living,* chapter II.

perversions, as they are more commonly called, some of them of a revolting nature. *"Every one who suffers from ereuthophobia,"* declares Stekel, *"has a bad conscience.* As the blushing of the chaste maiden is really an unconscious confession of her sexuality, so the blushing of the adult neurotic represents fear of "being found out!"[3]

Self-Consciousness, Not a Matter of Guilt

Now, we shall have no difficulty subscribing to the belief that all awareness of guilt in oneself tends to lower the threshold of self-consciousness; for in every social contact there appears to occur a reverberation of a suppressed fear, the thought "What if such-and-such should be known!" But in a sense, the theory begs the question; for in the last analysis, it amounts to simply this: self-conscious people are self-conscious because they are conscientious; for those who are unscrupulous, we know from common experience, will never be both-

---

[3] W. Stekel: *Condition of Nervous Anxiety and their Treatment,* p. 36.

ered about their private misdemeanors. But we have not yet been told why conscientious people should be self-conscious. Scrupulousness or conscientiousness, therefore, is only an attribute, not a cause of self-consciousness; and one must gather that both traits are dependent on a more basic quality. If the guilt complex were really at the root of this state of mind, then every gangster should turn crimson every time he showed his face, but as it happens, he is just the one who blushes least. On the contrary, I have seen some instances of excessive blushing in patients who are ethical far above the average and whose sense of guilt, in that case, can only be exaggerated under such conditions.

Stekel's contention, at first blush, seems to accord with the view of common sense. Since in daily life we blush when embarrassed because of some slip we have made, then all blushing must partake of that cowardly nature and must be evoked by that dynamic condition. The generalization, however, is not borne out in experience.

THEORIES OF SELF-CONSCIOUSNESS

Genitalization of Face

That blushing carries a sexual message, a confession of the libido urge, is more credible; and again it is Freud to whom the brilliant thought had occurred that when the erogenous zone (an erogenous zone is any part of the body which responds to sexual stimuli), is extended beyond its usual confines, the same physiological processes take place in the new territory as in the reproductive organs. Ferenczi,[4] one of Freud's most prominent followers, was under the impression that this genitalization takes place during the sublimation period in puberty.

Blushing and Sincerity

Similarly, Eisler,[5] of the same school, describes a case of ereuthophobia which was diagnosed as a conversion symptom, that is say a displacement from below, of exhibition in connection with self-abuse. Yet stage-fright is in-

---

[4] S. Ferenczi: *Further Contributions to the Theory and Technique of Psychoanalysis*, p. 85.

[5] J. Eisler: "Ein Fall von krankhafter Schamsucht." *Internat. Zeitsch f. Psychoanalyse*, vol. v, p. 41.

terpreted by Ferenczi[6] to be frequently the result of narcissistic splitting of the personality, so that the self might have a listener from within, which is only a symptom of an inner doubt about the sincerity of one's words. Now if Ferenczi had employed the word "faith," instead of "doubt" and "soundness" in the place of "sincerity," we could easily follow him, but to encumber the poor sufferer with another taint is only adding insult to injury, and that without the slightest justification.

The Psychoanalytic Viewpoint

It may be remarked in conclusion that the psychoanalyst does not look upon self-consciousness as a matter to study or treat as such. Indeed, I have not come across any allusions to this state or tendency except in connection with something more extensive and fundamental. Self-consciousness in psychoanalytic treatment is viewed much as a headache would be considered by a physician—merely a symptom of a more deep-seated ailment. The general

---

[6] S. Ferenzi: *loc cit.*, p. 421.

category under which psychoanalysts choose to subsume self-consciousness is *narcissism,* so affected as to give rise to an inferiority complex (not in Adler's but in Freud's sense of the term). The narcissistic person who, loosely speaking, is in love with himself, develops an "ego-ideal" which is rigorously watching over the "ego" or self—a glorified conscience, we may call it.

It is in Freud's essay "On Narcissism" that we find the following significant passage:

> Patients of this sort complain that all their thoughts are known and their actions watched and overlooked; they are informed by the functioning of this mental institution by voices which characteristically speak to them in the third person ("Now she is thinking of that again . . ." "Now he is going out"). This complaint is justified—it describes the truth; a power of this kind: watching, discovering and criticising all our intentions, does really exist; indeed it exists with every one of us in normal life.[7]

---

[7] S. Freud: "On Narcissism—an Introduction." *Collected Papers,* vol. IV. pp. 52-53.

Here then we have the genesis of self-consciousness in the psychoanalytic framework.

Blushing

Now that blushing has been mentioned, it is only natural that this highly human quality should receive a section by itself. It was no less a scientist than Charles Darwin who devoted a chapter to it in his *Expression of the Emotions in Man and Animals;* and much of what he brought out under that head still holds good today.

As a naturalist, he was able to compare humans and animals in that regard, and had established the fact that animals do not blush. To what extent savages blush is not clear. Differences in color make it somewhat difficult of comparison.

Darwin's Contribution

New circumstances and social attitudes have furnished the possibilities for testing out certain observations of Darwin and his associates, (Paget, Crichton Browne) *e.g.,* it would be

[160]

interesting to verify in nudist colonies the statement made by Darwin that blushing, with few exceptions, is restricted to those parts which are exposed. Even if it may be countered that nudism in civilized society is not a natural condition, and certainly not a permanent state, a certain tendency toward blushing elsewhere than in the face or neck should be noted, if Darwin's conclusion is correct.

While the author of the *Origin of Species* includes anecdote and particularly observations made by friends in his study, the results are in the main confirmed today, *e.g.*, as regards the movements and gestures which accompany blushing, the greater susceptibility of the young than the old and of women than men to this tendency. Darwin sums up his theory in these words:

> Blushing whether due to shyness—to shame for a real crime—to shame from a breach of the laws of etiquette—to modesty from humility—to modesty from an indelicacy—depends in all cases on the same principle; this

principle being a sensitive regard for the opinion, more particularly for the depreciation of others, primarily in relation to our personal appearance, especially of our faces; and secondarily, through the force of association and habit, in relation to the opinion of others on our conduct.[3]

It is rather significant that the celebrated naturalist makes personal appearance the basis of all blushing, this accounting for the fact that blushing is, as a rule, a function of the face only.

The core of Darwin's chapter, it must be said, consists in the physiological theory of blushing, explaining in detail the action of the capillary vessels, but for our purpose, it is not necessary to go into that part of the subject.

Blushing Wholesome

In popular lore blushing has always been regarded as a sign of wholesomeness. A hardened criminal, a brazen hussy has no longer the

---

[3] C. Darwin: *The Expression of the Emotions in Man and Animals,* pp. 335-336.

power to blush. This was very effectively brought out in the witty bull of the young woman who once admitted to her physician that the only thing she could blush for now is the fact that she couldn't blush for anything. The saying, which appears to have had its source in Cato's avowed preference, "A young man that blushes is better than one who turns pale" exemplifies the popular attitude in this respect.

The probability is, however, that there is not one type of blush, although through our inexpert eyes all blushes are rosy. Keats in his intuitive grasp perhaps comes closer to the truth when he sings:

> There's a blush for won't, and a blush for shan't
> And a blush for having done it
> There's a blush for thought and a blush for naught,
> And a blush for just begun it.

CHAPTER XI

He who thinks that only emotional stress and mortification akin to the state of fear is all that encumbers the "self-conscient," assuredly underestimates the trials and tribulations of such sufferers.

Ordeal of Self-Conscious People

In the first place, the personality of a self-conscious adult does not develop in the normal way. Distraction, absent-mindedness, a hesitant attitude both in gesture and in speech are among the consequences of this peculiar, though by no means rare form of "nervousness." The eyes become "stary." There is a tendency for the individual to shun the gaze of others, to look away when spoken to. The head often droops and a faulty posture is permanently established. Relations with acquain-

[164]

tances or strangers must seem forced. Lack of confidence is stamped all over the face and the man in the street is even apt to gain the impression of dishonesty from the roving eyes and furtive glance.

A Damper on Action

Furthermore, depression is likely to set in. The movements are retarded; and the greatest handicap in achievement where personal contact is essential is the lack of initiative and the generation of inhibitions which stifle action. Such people acquire the reputation of not being dependable in crucial moments, and will not be trusted with a task calling for quick action on the spur of the moment, even when there is no occasion for self-consciousness to arise; for, as the saying goes, "Give a dog a bad name and hang him."

The first one, at least in a Western language, to have given us a glimpse of the follies and deprivations of the self-conscious tribe was that prince of writers, Plutarch, whose essay *On Bashfulness* deals principally with the inhibitions which the shrinking person is subject to. "Thus in a dangerous fit of sickness we send not to the ablest physician, for fear of giving offence to another of our acquaintance . . . or, in our lawsuits, we do not see to it that we obtain qualified legal counsel, because we must gratify the son of some friend or relation, and give him an opportunity to show himself in the world." Plutarch teaches us not to allow ourselves to be imposed upon, to put people in their place, and learn to say "no" when it becomes necessary, either for our own good or in the interest of public policy, to refuse.

Self-Consciousness Retards Promotion

The vocational phase of self-consciousness has nowhere in the literature, or in the clinic, been adequately treated. An otherwise efficient teacher in a secondary school is in line for promotion to a mastership, but she becomes flustered when addressing her pupils, who scent this weakness even before she starts to speak, with the result that she cannot maintain discipline in the school. Should she be advised to give up administrative duties and appeal to the principal whenever a problem crops up, or should she be encouraged to fight the monster of self-consciousness until she is master of herself and mistress in the school? If there is no constitutional defect to deplete her energy, certainly the latter course is preferable as beneficial in the long run; for by solving her vocational problem she will also remove her personal handicap.

A Manager of People Should Not Be Self-Conscious

The manager, director, superintendent or even foreman is also called upon to exercise authority over subordinates, and unless he is self-composed, he cannot grapple with the situation in making his authority felt. A man may be dexterous with tools, skillful in his manipulations and thoroughly grounded in the principles underlying his job. Nevertheless he must in addition prove that he has gained that coolness and collectedness which brings about understanding in human relations.

In all social situations, adjustment is a requisite. Self-conscious people stall at the very outset, thus rendering their position static. Their emotional brooding interferes with action, and the greater the affection, the greater the inhibition.

Substituting Forwardness for Self-Consciousness

Sometimes a self-conscious individual will strike upon the idea of taking the bull by the horns and breaking through the reserve in which he is held, gripped as in a vise. While this is feasible and even advisable in or with one's family, or among companions, it becomes a risky business in approaching superiors. Those are the people who in their endeavor to overcome their impediment will fall into a predicament even more serious, namely, committing a rash act and appearing forward or rude.

Fancy the waiter who in order to disguise his nervousness when taking orders at a fashionable summer resort slaps his customer on the back, talks to him familiarly or speaks in a loud authoritative voice. The inhibition here has given way to an impulsion, but the remedy is even worse than the ailment. While it might have been said before that the waiter was a bit queer, it will now be concluded that he does not know his place, or that he is a boor.

Loss of Adjustment

In a youthful monograph on the interference of will impulses,[1] the author asked himself just what makes it so difficult for some persons to pass readily from one adjustment to another without tripping or staggering, and the answer suggested was that the difficulty lay in the excessive amount of imagination to which the inhibited individual is subject. In viewing fresh phases of a situation, particularly of a social type, perspective is lost because of the number of emotionally colored ideas crowding into the mental foreground. This imaginative flow prevents the "self-conscient" from getting his bearings. The motor attitude which is so essential in carrying out an act is not properly set, to begin with, so that the slightest change

---

[1] A. A. Roback: *The Interference of Will Impulses,* (Psychol. Monographs, 111) pp. 144-145.

[169]

in the total situation would be apt to throw out of gear the adjustment.

It is evident that the economy of imagination and association is most conducive to easy readjustment. Just enough is to be in consciousness as can be of aid in making the transition from one act to another. All the rest is irrelevant and defeats the end. Thus the speaker, who, when heckled by one of his listeners, attends only to the question and takes up a definite attitude, say of sarcasm, which brings on the desired associations, will probably manage to hold his own and carry his purpose. On the other hand, however, if he should begin wondering what right his interrupter had to ask the question, or whether he ought to rebuke him or reply in an agreeable tone, the previous adjustment is broken, and the next one must be started all anew.

Self-Consciousness, Not a Big Problem With Little Social Contact

Some occupations require less social contact than others, and therefore it is possible to guide those who are prone to become ill at ease in the presence of others into such vocations as would require few dealings with strangers. Even lawyers do not necessarily have to plead in court in order to make a decent livelihood. Technologists, clerks, bookkeepers, librarians, artisans, artists, and authors, have not much of a social demand on them in this connection. It goes without saying that even in such occupations, it is better to feel at home in company. But at any rate, it is comforting to know that there is relief to be had from the oppressing circumstances of an occupational environment.

Self-Consciousness, Not a Bar to Genius

Those who are called upon to perform in public: speakers, preachers, singers, instrumentalists, actors, etc., while they may show stage-fright in making their *début,* or appearing before an exceptionally critical or distinguished audience, learn in time to focus their attention on the performance. No matter how sensitive the artist is off the stage, he will always be able to exercise his self-control. After

[171]

all, we have not come across an orator or musician of high order whose self-consciousness has kept him from attaining renown in his chosen field, although not a few have been troubled with this affliction. Their talent and zeal conquer their shortcoming at least in their own sphere of endeavor, even if their nervousness remains with them in facing a public when not engaged in their special line of performance. Thus an orchestra conductor who never entertains a doubt about himself while directing the musicians with his baton, may appear paralyzed and blush crimson when he is expected to say a few words to the audience that greets him with an unusual ovation. Let us bear in mind that since one may be self-conscious in many different ways, there is a possibility of being "back-conscious" as well as "face-conscious." Now orchestra conductors, who have learned to make their backs immune from that affection, which otherwise, because of their exposure to the gaze of the public, should receive the brunt of their thought (in which case they would be "back-conscious"), may be in a peculiar con-

dition for the very reason of the displacement,
and hence the face, in the case of conductors,
may have become particularly sensitive.

Self-Consciousness In Different Phases of One's Personality

That self-consciousness may operate in partial
personality reactions, or constellations, can be
inferred from the circumstance that many an
individual, instead of displaying self-consciousness in someone's presence, will rather betray
it when *writing* to someone. The very same
person who is so much at ease, informal, and
even jolly in your company, may write you a
note which is stiff and stilted, as if you were a
perfect stranger or a slight acquaintance. The
handwriting may reveal slips and a tremor. Ob-
viously there is a speaking personality and a
writing personality; and why not then a singing or playing or acting personality, each
phase of which may be affected or not
according to the forte or foible, training
and compensation of the individual?

There are many people who become self-conscious when parting, saying "good-bye." They are quite at ease all the time of the conversation, but when it comes to break away, they become so nervous that they keep saying "Well—well—well—I guess it's time to go," and they show signs of confusion, sometimes even blush.

Entering a room or being introduced to people is fraught with self-consciousness for all sensitive people—one reason why it is so difficult to remember names after introductions—but that can be understood more readily than in the case of parting. And it is not so much a matter of thinking about the impression that is being left, because even with familiar friends, the parting goes hard; and much of the staircase or lobby farewell prattle is caused by this sort of self-consciousness, characteristic of more people than one ordinarily supposes.

Compensation In Self-Consciousness

It would not be fair to dwell on the vocational disadvantages of self-consciousness without mentioning at least one great advantage derived, to be sure, only through compensation in an indirect manner, nevertheless eventually a net gain. I am referring to the seclusion of self-conscious people, their shunning society and its time-consuming demands, with the result that those who withdraw into their own inner world and possess ability at the same time are in a position to accomplish a great deal more than the socially successful. They are less distracted by human relationships; they have more time at their disposal and can engage in contemplation so as to further their single purpose in life. Theirs is achievement, provided naturally they are not torn apart by conflict (social desires on the one hand and seclusion imposed by their failing on the other) or harrassed by the inhibitions incidental to their self-conscious tendency.

Vocational directors, at any rate, will do well to study their charges from the angle discussed in this chapter.

CHAPTER XII

The Treatment of Self-Consciousness

We finally come to the therapeutic aspect of self-consciousness, which is of course the most important stage in the study from the practical point of view. It will be necessary to recapitulate in this chapter some of the main results already affirmed and to refer to a number of the causes already dwelt on in another setting.

Wrong Attitude of Mind

It has been found that self-consciousness, except in those pre-psychotic stages which end in schizophrenia and paranoia, is neither a disease nor an ailment. It is merely a *wrong attitude* brought about by many causes. The introvert, whose thoughts and feelings are directed inwards instead of finding an outlet in contact with other people, is more apt to be self-conscious. The extravert, on the other hand, is not given to self-consciousness so much because his *self* is not exclusively his own; it is constantly assimilating the personalities with whom he comes in touch. Hence we may well say that constitutional and mental differences play a part in the determination of self-consciousness. But whereas many succeed in overcoming the difficulty, others do not. We must look into the reason which explains this different mode of development, and thus get to the core of our analysis.

Self-Consciousness, Associated With Feeling of Inferiority

It has already been shown that, very likely, self-consciousness *goes hand in hand with a feeling of inferiority in a certain respect.* The awkward youth, especially one who is not of a prepossessing appearance, will feel ill at ease in the presence of a beautiful and vivacious girl. The rounder, on the other hand, the man about town, will not let himself become confused. He "knows his onions" as they say in slang, and no matter how homely he may be, he realizes that his ammunition is a match for his fair companion. He meets his combatant on her own ground; and like the general who acquires the dash and authority of his presence by dint of the many battles he has fought, the man of the world treats everybody and everything only with a view to gaining his purpose.

Discrepancy Between Ambition and Achievement

Ordinary people who cherished ambitions in life which they never were able to realize seldom grow out of their self-consciousness, because back of their mind is the awareness that they have not made good, that their interlocutor or companion must surely be apprised of their shortcoming. As a matter of fact, prominent and really worth while men never stop to consider the history, mental conflicts, or inferiority feelings of those they speak to until these secrets are betrayed by the individuals themselves in their behavior.

As has already been implied, those who have achieved something in life, no matter in what walk, whether in finance or science, in music or industry, in sports or religion, will have gradually outgrown their self-consciousness. Several factors contribute to this salutary result. First, they are cognizant of a certain power, be it ever so much restricted; secondly, they are looked up to by others of their acquaintance, even if only by a circle of village inhabitants; thirdly, their intercourse with people will have given them a knack, so to speak, of handling situations.

Women Outgrow Self-Consciousness Sooner Than Men

The feeling of self-consciousness is, relatively speaking, outgrown at various ages. In men of the introverted type, the middle thirties should see the passing of this trait. In women of the same type fortunately this trait begins to wane in the early twenties. In spite of the accepted reserve and coyness of girls, there is less self-consciousness exhibited among them than among men much older, probably because coyness, which is a purposeful and sexualized self-consciousness, is one of the weapons at the disposal of girls in their battle for marriage.

[179]

SELF-CONSCIOUSNESS SELF-TREATED

It is generally thought that plain-looking girls and women are invariably self-conscious. Careful observation hardly bears this out, although I am willing to concede that the spinster complex in unmarried women is apt to intensify the feeling of self-consciousness. There are probably compensatory factors brought into play to offset the possible inferiority feeling. Many of these girls develop an animated expression, an interesting manner of conversation or a gracious bearing, a sympathetic approach that would put the prettier girl into the shade. An obliging attitude, kindness and a charitable point of view will do more to reduce the tendency toward self-consciousness.

Nervousness Seldom Completely Outgrown

Nor again must it be supposed that those who have established their reputation are never troubled by self-consciousness. Quite the contrary. Such men and women are sometimes weighted down with the thought that a great deal is expected of them, and more than once have I noticed a distinguished scholar mop his brow after delivering even a short address. There is a great liability inherent in this *noblesse oblige* attitude. Naturally a man of eminence should do his utmost not to disappoint, but the endeavors should have been made before the occasion at issue. The rest should be left to the efficient machinery of the subconscious mind. To worry about the audience at the critical moment interferes with the purpose of the speaker or performer.

Self-consciousness may arise on certain occasions even with those who ordinarily are cool and collected. Surely many of us have witnessed a meeting of two women who are leaders in their respective clubs and who can address large organizations without in any way feeling uncomfortable, and yet, because of a mutual distrust, they exhibit unmistakable signs of embarrassment.

Self-Consciousness, a Sign of Lack of Sympathy

Here we obtain another clue for an analysis. Sympathy and understanding are necessary for the maintenance of one's composure. When two people are of entirely different natures, both are at a loss as to how they will impress each other. Often a third person will earn the blessing of both by removing the barrier. But that is not all. The author is prepared to contend that *self-consciousness under such circumstances is a symptom of lack of broad sympathies.* The person who gains in worldly wisdom, who begins to take an intelligent interest in the welfare of his fellow-beings, will be surprised to find how much of his self-consciousness has disappeared. *Self-consciousness then is to some extent bound up with a lack of faith in others, with a certain aloofness from the world, an anticipation of hostility.*

Business and Society

Let us take another instance. A very successful salesman told the author that in a business way he is equal to approaching the most exalted person, but when he meets socially elevated people on other than business occasions, he is no longer his old self. He hesitates in speaking, he falters, makes awkward movements and experiences a rather general feeling of distress.

Apparently the commercial phase of his make-up found its counterpart in a certain phase of the other's personality, but socially he has not been able to acclimate himself to his superior's station of life. The bond of sympathy is missing there; and acquainted though the two people are, they seem to be strangers on the somewhat deeper levels.

Self-Centredness, Besetting Sin of Self-Consciousness

One's being conscious of oneself is not the only reason why the term "self-consciousness" has come into being as the most appropriate designation for the disturbing state of mind frequently referred to as "nervousness." The self is not only the object of consciousness in such instances. It is the stumbling-block in the path of efficiency. The self looms large in the mind of the self-conscious people, even though they may be and usually are altruistically inclined. The egocentricity or self-centredness in such individuals is not a quality of character, but a personality trait. We are not to understand that all self-centered persons are self-conscious, but merely that all "self-conscients" are self-centered, and it is from among the latter group that the diffident and nervous are recruited.

The self-conscious man thinks that he is so important that, in the first place, he is the cynosure of all eyes, and secondly, that his person must not be taken in vain by the slightest criticism. After he loses his somewhat distorted view which betrays a certain lack of insight, he gets rid also of a large dose of his self-consciousness.

Actually we are here in the realm of psychoanalysis; for what underlies such an attitude is what has been called "narcissism," which is defined in the *Dictionary of Psychology* as "the persistence of an early stage of psychosexual development, in which the sexual object, or love object remains the self."

As will be remembered, Freudians trace all self-consciousness to narcissism, even though

offhand it would seem that a person who is ill
at ease because he is not satisfied with himself
or his worth could not entertain such a high
opinion of himself as to be in love with his ego.
This, however, is not the only point in psychoanalysis which appears paradoxical to the layman; and offers no difficulty to anyone who is
acquainted with the concepts of *ambivalence,
reaction-formation,* and *duality,* the basic feature of which is that extremes meet, and that we
tend in the opposite direction from what really
ails us.

Selfish People May Not Be Self-Conscious

One might think that selfish people are more
mindful of themselves than the class of self-
conscious individuals, but this is probably due
to faulty interpretation on the part of the layman. The selfish person no more thinks of himself when engaging in his rapacious forays than
the wolf or bear is conscious of himself when
laying in wait for his prey. They are all conscious of their quarry or of their instinctive
urges, but the idea of the self as a cognitive

element or complex is never present in the animal and seldom does it arise in the appetitive economy of the selfish.

In the timid, the self is a barrier to success; in the aggressive it is a stepping-stone or bridge in order to arrive at their objective. The self-conscious person *thinks* about himself; the unconscientious individual (not that there is a real dichotomy intended between the two) *does* something with the self. Ordinarily, it is supposed that because the self-seeking are constantly thinking of their own interests, whenever they are about to carry out anything, the thought of the self is necessarily uppermost in their mind; but in the one sense, i.e., as applied to those who are aggressive, the self is a *proprietary domain from the angle of outsiders;* in the other, it is an *introspective* content.

Self-Confidence and Achievement

We must now start on our practical *résumé*. We have seen that pernicious self-consciousness arises out of a misguided idea concerning the relation between ourselves and others, that

the best way to overcome it is to build up a
sense of self-confidence and the best way to
gain self-confidence is to achieve something in
life. But while we are on the road to making
something of ourselves, we have to cope with
this drawback. What then is to be done?

Mix More With People

In the first place, we must mix more with the
world, even if it costs a great deal of effort.
The self-conscious individual cares more for his
own company than is good for him. This reclusiveness is not necessarily selfish, as we have
indicated. He would gladly feel free with
people if he could. But there is only one way
to break through the self that hinders him from
gaining poise and the sociability that every individual basically and psychologically needs,
and that is not by merely wishing it, but by in-
augurating a program of rubbing elbows with
others and forcing oneself to like it.

Adopt a Spontaneous Attitude

The James-Lange doctrine of emotions,
which would make our feelings depend on

what goes on in our blood vessels and body in general, could be well utilized in our present problem. Even though it has been impugned as a theory of what happens when we are emotionally excited, we can still avail ourselves of the practical value of such a motor theory by impressing upon ourselves the fact that in order to become free from self-consciousness and even immune to it, we must *act* even though there is at first no spontaneity to what we are doing, that is to say, we must go through all the gestures and work toward cultivating even the intonation of those who are not self-conscious; in other words, *act* to establish the mental set of spontaneity.

Prophets, agitators of all kinds, reformers, politicians and promoters, more particularly, and all those who are intensely interested in the measures they are proposing are never troubled by self-consciousness. It behooves us at critical times to *act* the fanatic, the crank, the zealot just as a mild poison or narcotic is sometimes prescribed as an antidote for a more virulent drug. Once we have freed ourselves from the shackles of self-consciousness, we can easily regain our conservative equilibrium.

Maintain a Firm Belief in Your Message

The ruling thought should always be: "Those people to whom I am talking must accept my suggestion"—not, "I wonder how they are taking my 'spiel'!" It was this attitude which carried the author through in his first talk before the microphone, although he did not have a single word of his lecture written down. Perhaps as many as a hundred thousand were listening in, but that idea did not occupy his mind. The message was uppermost. We should take a decided stand, begin to speak as if what we are going to say is important, instead of mumbling it; and above all, work up a faith in our message or work.

Anyone who witnessed this first performance before the microphone would scarcely associate the speaker with the extremely self-conscious student of a dozen years ago; for well do I remember with what trepidation and palpitation I would stand before a person of note. In a seminar with other graduate students, I could never make my point in discussing a fellow student's paper. I had a feeling that my argument was scarcely worth giving, that others surely have anticipated it, that the famous man who directed the seminar was not interested in that particular question, and so forth. Naturally I spoke without gusto, and my words were scarcely audible. Whatever I said was lost. No impression was made, and I was only confirmed in the belief that my powers of oral discussion were not much above the zero mark. All I needed was to change the content of my belief, and with it my attitude—to suppose that my interjection was important, that most of the listeners were waiting to get more light on the subject, and that some were even eager to have the student reading the seminar-paper criticized.

Thus it is with anything else we can think of. There are people who can actually sing when no one is listening to them, although such a statement is considered to be a confession of inability. No sooner is the singer or player aware of someone's presence, especially if that someone is not a sympathetic relative, than the knack is gone and cannot be recalled.

Self-Consciousness Is Not Suddenly Eliminated

It is understood of course that self-consciousness will not disappear in a jiffy by some hocus-pocus even of a trained psychologist or neurologist. The individual's coöperation is always absolutely necessary. Exercises to suit different individuals may be devised by the therapist. In case of stage-fright, for example, the patient may be allowed at first to play or sing with others, then, by gradually reducing the number of fellow-players, to perform as a soloist.

Suggestion, whether in the normal waking state or during hypnosis, is of great benefit. Something of a psychoanalytic transference is to be aimed at by the therapist in order to bring about lasting results.

To tell the "self-conscient" that he must say to himself constantly, "Now, I must not be self-conscious any more," is just about as efficacious

as the Coué auto-suggestive couplet, "Day by
day, in every way, I'm getting better and better," when people haven't the least idea of the
meaning of right thinking. Not maxims but
good honest reflection and effort are requisite
for the banishing of nervousness. That the underlying dynamic causes are to be looked into
all the while, goes naturally without saying.

An Archbishop's Story

It will be highly instructive to look into the
manner in which Archbishop Whately cured
himself of what might be considered a troublesome case of self-consciousness. He did not
have to resort to psychoanalysis or consult a
psychiatrist, even if such recourses were available then, but simply took himself in hand, observed the situation, compared himself with
other people, and re-educated himself to the extent of becoming a shining example to others in
social matters. Smiles tells us that when the
young churchman and logician was at Oxford
"his white, rough coat and white hat obtained
for him the sobriquet of 'The White Bear'; and

his manners, according to his own account of himself, corresponded with the appellation. He was directed, by way of remedy, to copy the example of the best mannered men he met in society; but the attempt to do this only increased his shyness, and he failed. He found that he was all the while thinking of himself, rather than of others; whereas thinking of others, rather than of one's self, is of the true essence of politeness.

"Finding that he was making no progress, Whately was driven to utter despair; and then he said to himself, 'Why, should I endure this torture all my life to no purpose? I would bear it still if there were any success to be hoped for; but since there is not, I will die quietly, without taking any more doses. I have tried my very utmost, and find that I must be as awkward as a bear all my life, in spite of it. I will endeavor to think as little about it as a bear, and make up my mind to endure what can't be cured.' From this time forth he struggled to shake off all consciousness as to manner, and to disregard censure as much as possible.

[193]

In adopting this course, he says: 'I succeeded beyond my expectations; for I not only got rid of the personal suffering of shyness, but also of most of those faults of manner which consciousness produces; and acquired at once an easy and natural manner—careless, indeed, in the extreme, from its originating in a stern defiance of opinion, which I'had convinced myself must be ever against me; rough and awkward, for smoothness and grace are quite out of my way, and, of course, tutorially pedantic; but unconscious, and therefore giving expression to that good-will towards men which I really feel; and these, I believe, are the main points. "

Special Devices

That there are certain obstinate cases of self-consciousness cannot be denied. At times it is necessary to recommend special devices. It is even advisable to force the issue and make a mental incision, not unlike that of a surgical operation. In a class of several hundred students, the author asked how many of the members were generally self-conscious. Of course many hands went up. Then it was asked how many were extremely self-conscious so as to be constantly bothered. Only a few hands went up this time, although it may well have been that the one who was abnormally self-conscious, was even too self-conscious to raise his hand, just as in a certain laziness contest, when the competing group were asked which one of them was laziest, all but one raised their hands. "And you," said the judge to the individual who did not raise his hand, "are you not lazy?" "Well," answered the exception with a drawl and a yawn, "I am too lazy to move my hand."

At any rate, one of the few self-confessed bashful people was selected and ordered to come to the platform. Reluctantly he drew forward. A few words were whispered to him, and after a few pertinent questions, he was asked to address the class. He blushed and stood atremble, but the injunctions given him previously apparently did their work, for soon he stood erect, the face flushed no longer, and the

next moment he was telling about an occurrence, in a composed manner, finishing the
story amidst the applause of the audience.
That person, who, by the way, was not a young
student, had passed the crisis. It was perhaps
a drastic measure to take, and some might even
call it a "mean trick," but the end, in this case
at least, justified the means.

Picking Out Flaws In Others

Sometimes it is beneficial for the self-conscious person to "size up" others for a flaw or
two so as to counterbalance the fancied superiority of the individual which unwittingly calls
forth the self-consciousness. It is better not to
dwell on this, for it is a rather dangerous practice to be recommended only in stubborn individual cases—dangerous because criticism of
this deliberate sort is the foundation of the inferiority complex and is bound to magnify
whatever tendency we have of this nature.

It is, however, quite safe to say that thinking
about others, "sizing them" up without making them notice the fact, observing matters in

general would tend to divert attention from oneself. You cannot, in other words, think about yourself and about others with equal intensity at the same time.

Diet and Hygiene

It is customary in psychotherapeutic treatises to devote some space to diet and hygiene; and almost invariably we are told that in such and such a disorder, rest and good food, air, exercise and frequent bathing should be prescribed. It seems as if the regimen is the same in every case, which is always an indication of perfunctoriness on the part of the writer. Since it is accepted in medical circles that drugs and stimulants are not beneficial to the human organism, this consideration is always thrown in for good measure, the thought behind it being that certainly such an admonition can do no harm.

Stimulants May Be Helpful, But Not to Be Depended Upon

With regard to self-consciousness, all that may be said is this: everything which makes for a higher standard in life should be followed, because there is a greater chance then of assimilation to one's fellow-beings, and consequently less danger of excessive individualization or leading a reclusive life as a shut-in personality. But as far as stimulants are concerned, the author, for one, fails to see wherein the self-conscious individual aggravates his case very much by partaking of stimulants. On the contrary, it is likely that a mild stimulant lifts the spell and gives the timid a bit more self-confidence. But one should not depend too much upon stimulants. There is scarcely any emotional experience the intensity of which will not be either greatly increased or considerably diminished through the agency of some drug; yet only under the most unusual circumstances should a drug be prescribed or taken either to generate a desirable emotion or to alter the course of an undesirable one. Sedatives, on the other hand, are not to be recommended, except where the state of self-consciousness has turned into an access of excitement, which changes the total situation.

The Question of Smoking

The question whether smoking is of benefit to "self-conscients" is usually answered in the affirmative, because this habit is said to exercise a calming effect. At least that is the consensus of smokers. This opinion may, however, be called into question. Any physical activity is likely to release mental tension; and there is probably no more curative value in smoking than in eating, drinking, gum chewing, or bathing. The act of lighting a cigarette or cigar, like removing the peel from a banana or the tinfoil from a piece of chocolate, gives one that anticipatory satisfaction which goes with every gratification of a desire, and because smoking is often a social pastime and boasts of a technique (striking the match or the lighter, applying it to the tobacco, flicking the ashes, puffing the smoke, producing rings) there has developed an air of indifference and coolness just as in the process of angling. Hence the oft quoted advertising slogan about the nonchalance displayed in lighting a cigarette. However, real calmness or indifference is not *displayed*. Certainly I should not advise self-conscious non-smokers to start smoking as a cure for their nervousness or timidity. If, however, one does find by experience that smoking is a help in an emergency and that the nonchalance and self-satisfaction that smokers exhibit tend to relieve the strain, then by all means, the remedy should be resorted to.

Dancing, on the other hand, because of the rhythmic movements which the individual must go through, is decidedly of value in fighting *gaucherie* and the state of mind which brings it about. Furthermore dancing removes the barrier between the sexes which self-conscious young people set up.

Even driving an automobile gives a feeling of power and confidence that is an aid in solving the problem. Of course the process of learning is often fraught with embarrassment and awkwardness, whatever the activity, but as soon as progress is evident, the achievement begins to affect the individual favorably.

TREATMENT OF SELF-CONSCIOUSNESS

Plutarch's Lesson

It may seem more than antiquated to consult a writer who lived nearly two thousand years for advice on bashfulness, yet such authors as Plutarch are always modern in spirit, especially as in the rule he suggests to conquer this "distemper," as he calls it, he invokes the principle of mental association (vividness) which, looked at from another angle, is the influential conditioned reflex theory.

> Whenever they have given way to this weakness, let them store up carefully such failings in their memory and taking therein deep and lively impressions of that remorse and disquiet they occasioned, bestow much time in reflecting upon them and keeping them fresh. For as travellers that have got a dangerous fall against such a stone, or sailors shipwrecked upon a particular promontory, keeping the image of their misfortune continually before them, appear fearful and apprehensive not only of the same but even of similar dangers, so they that keep in

mind the disgraceful and prejudiced effects of bashfulness will soon be enabled to restrain themselves in like cases, and will not easily slip again on any occasions.

The American reflexologists will probably reply to this "You're darn tootin' they will. Their previous disagreeable experiences will condition their bashfulness or self-consciousness all the more."

Courage, Best Remedy for Self-Consciousness

Above all, nevertheless, it should be borne in mind that mental control and self-discipline on the basis of rational conclusions and insight gained through social contact will be of far greater consequence than all the nostrums and panaceas that may be devised. One ounce of spontaneous will is worth more than a pound of artificial "fixing."

'Difficile est, fateor, sed tendit in arduà virtuts.'[1]

---

[1] "It is difficult, I confess, but virtue tends in the direction of hardship."

CHAPTER XIII

THE EXPERIMENTAL PSYCHOLOGY OF SELF-CONSCIOUSNESS

Difficult to Experiment With Emotion

The difficulty of introducing experimental methods in the field of affection or in feeling and emotion is all too well known among psychologists. The so-called expressive methods in which instruments like the sphygmograph, plethysmograph, pneumograph, and the like are employed for the purpose of correlating the rapidity of the pulse-beat, the volume of blood, or the rate of breathing with the course of a particular emotion, are not entirely satisfactory, partly because of the faulty technique inherent in such "rig-ups" and partly due to the impossibility of interpreting with certainty a given state of consciousness on the basis of records derived from the application of these methods.

[203]

The Expressive Methods of Experimentation

The psychogalvanometer, which measures the emotional tone of an individual by means of a weak electrical current passed through the body and registering on a scale, is a more satisfactory piece of apparatus, from the technical standpoint, but in spite of its standing with some authorities, it is still in the promising stage.

Of late, many claims have been made for the sphygmomanometer as a detector of the lying consciousness, but from personal knowledge as an observer in such experiments, the author would say that there is much to be desired in the way of satisfactory results even in the task of exposing the lying *consciousness,* let along the infinitely greater enterprise of ''nailing a lie.''

Paradox of Experiment

The comparative inaccessibility of the affective states to experimental control may be readily understood when we consider that an emotion, in order to retain its essence, must be spontaneous. An artificial stimulus mars

[204]

the process from the beginning, and as for introspection, even the sage of ages ago who was responsible for the wholesome advice to count ten when angry and one hundred when very angry, knew that cognition and affection cannot run along parallel to each other. Hence to study oneself while angry, or in fear, results in studying not one's anger or fear but some other state, transitional from the affective to the cognitive.

Psychoanalytic Method of Getting at Emotion

Such were the drawbacks of this most important department in psychology until the dynamic system inaugurated by Freud and his psychoanalysis did away with all attempts at experimentation and began to focus attention on the hidden complexes. While engaged in this endeavor, Jung stumbled on the association method, already in vogue among criminologists, and elaborated his technique for discovering personality traits directly responsible for certain neuroses. Self-centredness or egocentricity, as a matter of fact, is one of the fundamental characteristics tapped by this method, but egocentricity is not the same thing as self consciousness, although there may be a correlation between the two.

The Traditional Experimentalist, Still Persistent

The traditional psychologist with his hankering for experimental procedure was not, however, prepared to leave the field completely to psychoanalysis. Thanks to his ingenuity, tests were devised by which emotional attitudes could be investigated and emotional reactions artificially produced. It seemed after all relatively easy to rub a student "the other way" and then to study his demeanor, facial expression, words, etc., and even his introspective content.

Methods and Technique

The state of self-consciousness is an emotional frame of mind and, therefore, possesses all the difficulties which emotion in general exhibits. We may rule out, to begin with, the expressive methods, as their inadequate character has already been alluded to. What remains is this:

(a) To study the self-conscious individual objectively in a given situation.

(b) To ask the individual to describe his state of mind in detailed form.

(c) To produce situations for the express purpose of inducing the state of self-consciousness in generally immune individuals.

(d) To examine physiologically various internal processes and secretions before, approximately during, and after the onset.

(e) To compare complex mechanized movements (as in writing, playing, etc.) in the self-conscious and the non-self-conscious states.

(f) To extend the association method, adapting it so as to bear especially upon self-consciousness.

Some of these methods require no explanation. Their mode of application will occur to anyone trained in the laboratory. Others need a word or two of comment.

No Objection to Inducing Self-Consciousness

The means of inducing self-consciousness are not nearly so objectionable as in the case of calling forth fear or anger; and furthermore, while the effects of artificial fright may be deleterious to the subject, the cumulative results of induced self-consciousness are, for the most part, beneficial in that there is a gradual weaning away from the state, the individual becoming tolerant to certain situations which in the past would have been troublesome.

Non-Social Stimuli

What, in the rough, is the technique of bringing about self-consciousness? Numerous devices may be thought of. Requiring the subject to look into a mirror is a simple experimental task. Few individuals can avoid preening when they stand before a mirror. Similarly posing before a camera is a favorable situation for the purpose. In perhaps seven out of every ten photographs, the stamp of self-consciousness is unmistakably visible. Yet this self-consciousness is probably more akin to the ego-consciousness spoken of earlier in the treatment. There is a narcissistic element, a marked tendency toward self-admiration displayed in this type of self-consciousness, which does not involve the social presence.

Descriptive Observation

Although scattered observations on bashfulness were to be found here and there in text books and treatises, such as Darwin's *The Expression of the Emotions in Man and Animals,* it was the pioneer spirit of G. Stanley Hall, responsible also for the introduction of the questionnaire as a psychological method, that stimulated inquiry along these lines.

In 1895, Hall distributed a questionnaire on "Some Common Automatisms and Nerve Signs." Among many of the questions asked were the following:

> How do you know you are going to blush? Where is it first felt? Do you feel it in hands, arms, limbs, neck,

[209]

chest? Are there attendant tweaks, tingles, twinges, or other sensations, elsewhere, or any reaction of pallor or chill? Describe spontaneous flushes in any part of the body as when alone. Teasing to make others blush. Describe your own blushing habits and those of your friends.

G. E. Partridge[1] in collating the results stresses the variety of causes, and, in general corroborates the observations by Darwin.

A much more extensive study on "Showing Off and Bashfulness as Phases of Self-Consciousness,[2] deals with the observed behavior of children from infancy to puberty; and in a few cases, of adults. It is worth noting that the behavior was incidental to both ego-consciousness and self-consciousness. Both the age and the sex of the youngsters was given as well as the circumstances and the acts (running away, hiding the face, fidgety movements, awk-

---

[1] G. E. Partridge: "Blushing." *Pedag: Seminary,* 1897, vol. IV.

[2] G. S. Hall and T. L. Smith: "Showing off and Bashfulness as Phases of Self-Consciousness." *Pedag. Seminary,* 1903, vol. X.

wardness, blushing, giggling, inhibitions and lapses of speech, manual inefficiency, inability to eat). Here we have the raw data of the child's ego.

These listings of observations were scorned by psychologists in Hall's time as unproductive of results. To be sure, an inventory cannot take the place of a dynamic theory or conclusion, but without an inventory, our theories may be only barren hypotheses.

Social Passive Situation

Self-consciousness will best lend itself to study when the individual is suddenly confronted with a person who is regarded as a superior. If the experimenter has arranged beforehand with the head of the department, or the dean, or the college president, to enter lightly without knocking, during the experimental period, the scene has already been laid. For variations, a prominent man in the community, a noted actor or better still, a pretty actress would yield the desired results. Increase in numbers is frequently an added incentive for self-consciousness to arise.

[211]

SELF-CONSCIOUSNESS SELF-TREATED

Social Active Situation

While the above method enjoys the advantage
that the predicament for the subject requires
fortitude, there is little resistance encountered.
The more advanced step of having the subject
participate in some activity (singing, reciting)
before admired visitors brings us to a more
critical stage of the experimental procedure, to
be taken only with the tough-minded, who seldom become embarrassed. The strong resistance offered, as well as the possibly partial re-
sentment shown, are all phases of the state of
self-consciousness, which must be noted down
in detail.

No Experimentation With Self-Consciousness

The experimental psychology of self-consciousness is, in a sense, more important than
experimentation on certain types of imagery or
the dimensions of feeling-tone, because in the
sphere of self-consciousness, we are concerned
not only with explanations of the state, but also
with the problem of therapy or cure. And yet
there is scarcely any need of stating that the

suggestions here have never, to my knowledge, been put into use—in other words, there is nowhere any reference in the psychological literature to experiments on self-consciousness, aside from those on animals adverted to in the early part of this book. It is only for this reason that I venture to set down the few considerations which must strike the reader as extremely schematic. My object is rather to point out the fact that this strip of psychological territory has been neglected, than to outline the possibilities which practically every psychologist can perceive for himself. There is no doubt that more minuteness in each of the methods suggested is a desideratum which, however, is bound to realize itself in the course of the experimental procedure—a case of the dinner growing with the appetite.

It is my belief that in the near future, the field of self-consciousness will receive more attention from educators, who are inclined in general to treat the condition as a passing state which can do no harm, and which many of themselves had to go through. Here is a peculiarly human tendency and one which means so much to an individual from a practical point of view, and yet even those who are in charge of the youth: principals, superintendents, vocational counsellors do not make much ado about it, although the funds necessary for surveys and a thoroughgoing investigation would by no means equal the enormous appropriations called for in other scientific or educational projects.

CHAPTER XIV

SUMMARY

Next to the depression, I should say that most people are suffering from self-consciousness, but while depression affects mainly the poor, self-consciousness affects both poor and rich, chiefly the younger people.

It is one of the paradoxes of our educational system that while millions feel the pinch of self-consciousness, there is an incredible dearth of material on the subject, as if there were a conspiracy of silence on this matter. Adolescents are supposed to get over it just as the children do the measles, teething, and other necessary passing ailments. The self-conscious person is too self-conscious to make a fuss, and the non-self-conscious individual cannot bring himself to believe that there are such "simps," who cannot answer an ordinary question without mopping their brow from embarrassment.

SELF-CONSCIOUSNESS SELF-TREATED

Self-consciousness is not merely thinking of one's self. There are those conceited egos who are always aware of themselves whenever they speak, move, smoke, walk; and, in their smug complacency, are virtually saying to themselves, "What a fine impression I'm making!"

"Will B, at least concede my skill?" "Clare will have to admit that I am wonderful." Sometimes, this attitude of self-elation is thought to be self-consciousness. Generically speaking, this is true, but in order to avoid confusion, let us rather call this "ego-consciousness" and restrict the term self-consciousness to the feeling or supposition that one is the object of observation by others with a view to criticism. In other words, the self-conscious person is always afraid that he is watched for every slip, every wrong gesture, every vocal inflection, etc.

Naturally the first question that will occur to one is: Why should we be self-conscious? This question may be analyzed or elaborated into the following:

"Am I really inadequate that I should feel so in the presence of others?"

SUMMARY

"Why is it that X, Y, Z, who has just enough brains to fill the cavity of a tooth should act with such self-possession and poise?"

"Is self-consciousness a disease, an abnormal state, or a healthy sign of the transition period?"

"What types of people are self-conscious?"

We must get at the causes of self-consciousness.

Let me begin by pointing out that self-consciousness is a human trait. Animals do not reveal any traces of this malady. Furthermore, very young children do not show any sign of self-consciousness. Bashfulness seldom appears earlier than the sixth month of life. Elderly people are not given to this mental state, and where such preoccupation with one's self is observable, the chances are that the individual is developing ideas of a pathological nature—in this case, *ideas of reference, i.e.,* a belief that others are referring to him, laughing at him, condemning him, and what-not. Such ideas are perilously near the boundary line between sanity and insanity.

On the other hand, there is something whole-some about self-consciousness. Self-conscious-ness is the setting for the jewel of conscience. It is the early and superficial distinguishing mark of dreamers, artists, men and women of imagination, mental aristocrats, the tender-minded as against the tough-minded. Most— not some, as the horoscope lingo goes, but most —of our great have been self-conscious in their youth, even the redoubtable Napoleon, not to speak of writers, composers, painters, scien-tists, and businessmen. Those very steel mag-nates, oil kings, department store lords who have climbed to the very pinnacle of fame were at one time shy and confused in the presence of their superiors. Autobiography teems with passages disclosing the silly wretchedness of the author, who, had there been some mentor to advise him, would have been spared a good deal of misery. Yes, and he would doubtless have missed a certain amount of poetry. With-out going into the issue as to whether the bene-fit is commensurate with the pain, it must needs be said that poetry cannot grow on soil which has not been irrigated first by the discomfiture of self-consciousness.

What Are We Self-Conscious About?

When we are beset by self-consciousness, we are comparing ourselves with someone else whom we think superior in a certain respect; and we begin thinking about our imperfection as viewed by another or others. We are more frightened when in a group, because we imagine that the criticism there will be multiplied. The poor and shabby will feel awkward in the presence of the rich. (Of course political views and the situation of the world today will materially affect this fact.) The homely will blush in the presence of the beautiful or handsome of the opposite sex. Those of poor physique will have in mind the thought that the well set-up interlocutor is pitying them or rating them as inferior. Remove the company and the self-consciousness is gone. If you are self-conscious when no one is about, then you are fostering a state of morbid introspection.

Comparatively few are bothered to that extent; and we have not touched on the neurosis of self-consciousness yet.

Everyone is familiar with the illustrations of self-consciousness. We may sing tolerably well in the bath tub when the family is away and we say to ourselves, "Now if I just can muster up enough courage to strike the same tones when friend-wife is in." But you try on a given occasion, and the funny sound you emit shocks even you, while the "missus" looks up and asks you whether you have a frog in the throat, and as for the children they greet your musical attempt with titters or even peals of laughter. You belong to the vast army of those who can sing when no one is listening, who have graceful gestures when no one is looking on, who could even play golf well, if your fellow player did not observe you.

You can experiment for yourself. Walk behind someone you know and admire, and you walk like a major. Walk in front of the same person and you begin to straighten up, assume an artificial attitude, perhaps even waddle a bit and you heave a sigh of relief when you have reached your destination.

The Nervous Mechanism of Self-Consciousness

Why does a mere thought affect us so as to put us out of gear? In order to give an adequate reply to this question, it would be necessary to illustrate by means of diagrams showing the operations that take place in the nervous system incidental to any bit of behavior. For want of space, however, and also because charts might appear too technical here, we need only refer to a rough sketch given in chapter IV, where the shunting, derailing, or telescoping of nerve impulses representing the particular act aimed at by the interloping idea of being watched, actually tells the story.

Failure and Self-Consciousness

Although thoroughly acquainted with the tribulations of self-consciousness from first hand sources, I was quite surprised to learn from any university extension classes that very many of the students had considered this their greatest handicap in life. Perhaps they have exaggerated somewhat, and possibly self-consciousness is one of the alibis to cover a multitude of shortcomings, but nearly everyone can remember how some fear of criticism or scorn had been an impeding factor in his advancement.

We make up our mind to talk to the boss about promotion or an increase in salary. Fully determined of our course, we knock at the door of the office, hear the boss's "come" with a thumping heart, go over our little "say" in our mind, but the employer's quizzical or impatient look frustrates our plan. We become self-conscious. We begin to speak, the voice is either hollow or high-pitched. Our posture is comical. The boss looks not only puzzled but even knits his brow (a strategic device of bosses). We hem and haw and finally deem ourselves fortunate if we can think up something in connection with our work, such as that the machine needs repairing, or the quality of the material needs looking into.

SUMMARY

To suitors, self-consciousness has been a veritable bane. Even in our age of speed, there will be found many boys and girls who vacillate and hesitate because they have in mind their dignity, their pride, their possibly being refused, etc. Indeed there is a species of impotence which is due to nothing more serious than self-consciousness.

Actors and actresses are not immune to self-consciousness. In fact, one of the most marked types of this trouble is what is called "stage-fright." It only goes to show that stage people are imaginative, and the fear of making a flop grips them just as it would an ordinary person. Virtuosi of the piano or violin have been known to undergo torture before their first public performance, and in more than one instance has failure been due to self-consciousness. It stands to reason that any nervous impulse which obtrudes itself against the machinery in the nervous system necessary for the bringing about of the most skillful movements must ruin the playing.

SELF-CONSCIOUSNESS SELF-TREATED

Severe Cases of Self-Consciousness

While most people are self-conscious on occasion, there are some whose self-consciousness has become a dread affliction, an obsession like any other obsession. They are constantly perturbed. If their employer comes into their office or visits the plant they begin to fidget incessantly, beads of perspiration roll down their forehead, their mouth becomes dry, all their muscles tense. Should they be asked to take dictation then, their fingers will tremble, their lips will quiver, they will grow purple in the face, make one mistake after another in their shorthand, and sometimes will even burst out crying as the only relief.

Efficiency and self-consciousness do not go hand in hand. At the time of our working, there is only one place for our self and that is to be immersed in the work. Fancy an acrobat or juggler thinking about himself when engaged in his stunts. The least mental deviation from the task in hand may cost him his job, if not his life. In considering the treatment of self-consciousness, it is well to ponder on the mutual exclusion of the ideas of self and work. But this leads us to the very nubbin of our subject —the remedy for this scourge.

The Cure for Self-Consciousness

Since self-consciousness is a state which depends on one or more of several different factors, one of which is at least hereditary and the other circumstantial or environmental, there can scarcely be one definite formula suggested. As a rule, the self-conscious are born with a predisposition to overvalue their personal dignity. The source then seems to be hereditary. There are two forces at work in such individuals: they are not sure of their ability or other qualities which count, and at the same time, they are proud. Socially they may feel inferior, and yet intrinsically they know themselves to be superior, but what crushes them is that others will not recognize this superiority.

A thick-skinned person will not be much concerned about possible criticism at the hands of a stranger. The "self-conscient" (a word which must be coined in view of the wide application of the subject) is sensitive, reads much more into the words or acts of his fellow-beings than there is in reality, frequently misconstrues, shows his touchiness by sulking or by "having it out" with a more or less close friend. One misunderstanding leads to another and the state becomes chronic, ready to become active at the slightest or even no provocation.

One of the chief faults of self-conscious people (and I am speaking of adults who have not yet gotten over their trouble) is their unwillingness to mix, their aloofness, their insistence on their own exclusiveness. That little bridge which connects human beings in everyday life is missing. Instead of a smile or sympathetic glance, a forbidding face, or a quizzical look announces to all newcomers that here is an unapproachable.

The self-conscient regards himself as a world in himself and all the rest as belonging to another world. Every statement, every gesture to him is fraught with significance and becomes a problem. The most ordinary request, the simplest question of a clerk in a store gives rise to a quandary. Should he say: "What do you ask for this"? "What does this cost?" or "What do you charge for this"? or perhaps "What's the price of this"? Again and again, he considers in his own mind as to which would be the most fitting form, when what he should have done is to banish all such casuistry and pedantry from his system and let himself be guided by just the impulse to ask the price.

As he reduces the distance between himself and others, his self-consciousness begins to disappear. When he creates a *social atmosphere,* he effects an implicit understanding between himself and others. It is harder to do this with some than with others. When "self conscient" meets "self-conscient", nothing can be done about it. We have all heard the story about the Englishman who was drowned because his fellow-Englishman, bathing close by, would not think of attempting to save someone he was not formally introduced to.

One of the natural remedies of self-consciousness is success in life. An employer is never self-conscious in the presence of an employee, unless of course there is a love relationship involved. A physician is not self-conscious when examining a patient, although if he stutters or betrays some nervous habit he may become self-conscious on noticing the patient's observance. Prosperity, age, experience—all these will aid the self-conscient to throw off the incubus, but his own individual effort is worth more.

Faith in Our Message

Perhaps a better piece of advice to the self-conscious is to bear in mind their message, to be earnestly preoccupied with the task they have to carry out, and there will be no room for self-consciousness. Have faith in your own words, and no amount of criticism will shake you. Disraeli was perhaps the most jeered statesman of his day, but I doubt whether he was ever bothered with self-consciousness, though there was possibly a dose of ego-consciousness in his make-up.

The worst feature of the self-conscious is that they shrink at the very thought of speaking to a stranger, or making a public address, asking for a job, or doing anything which they have not been in the habit of performing socially and which is, therefore, distasteful to them. It requires some grit or guts to make a beginning. At first, the endeavor may appear crude, awkward, but gradually more spontaneity will be attained.

In a university extension class of approximately a thousand students, I once picked out a self-conscious young man and asked him to mount the platform. Reluctantly he came forward blushing and blanching alternately. In suggestive and sympathetic tones, I cajoled him into relating something to the eager class. He nearly staggered for a moment, but the suggestion took effect. He calmed down, straightened, cleared his throat and began to speak, at first in a falsetto voice, and then in a more natural strain until he seemed to speak quite spontaneously, earning the applause of the mammoth class at the close of his little story. The operation was irksome, but successful, and the young man undoubtedly has broken the neck of his resistance.

SELF-CONSCIOUSNESS SELF-TREATED

It is of course more difficult to operate on oneself, but we can resolve determinedly to "speak up" the next time we have something to say, and when the time comes we must, under no circumstances, ask for a reprieve or postponement, but take our courage in both hands. The next time the "going" will be much easier, until in a short period we shall speak or act in company without any strain. The time to train ourselves is *before* the event calling for action. We form what is called a "mental set." The rest follows of its own accord. The habit—and in a sense self-consciousness may be called a habit—is destroyed.

There are no nostrums, no panaceas, no specifics for the most universal, although fortunately the mildest, of all mental ills. Let your message take hold of you so as to submerge your self. Pay little heed to *possible* criticism. Take up an attitude as if a certain result depended on *your* words or action. Make the other fellow believe that you have understood him and that for the moment, at any rate, you are on the same level. Avoid all tension except as a means of expression. Do the above and your problem is solved.

What has been said about love, *viz.*, that "it is better to have loved and lost than never to have loved at all" may perhaps be applied to the state of self-consciousness, except that in the former case, the stress is on the positive fact of the *loving,* while in the latter, the stress is on the *losing.* In both cases, however, not to have had the experience is to have missed something which goes to round out one's personality.

APPENDIX

NOTE:—In order to gain an idea of how much of the book you have assimilated, ascertain how many questions taken up in this volume, you can answer without consulting the text. The last few questions are problems which require an independent approach.

QUESTIONS COVERED IN THIS BOOK

1. What is the philosophical meaning of self-consciousness?

2. What is the popular meaning of self-consciousness?

3. How much is this popular meaning of the phrase adopted in literature?

4. How much of a problem is self-consciousness?

5. What is the difference between ego-consciousness and self-consciousness?

6. How many people out of a thousand think that their greatest personal handicap is self-consciousness?

7. Show why self-consciousness is not limited to one type of mind?

8. Into what two general divisions will the subject of self-consciousness be divided in our scheme?

9. How can the subjective state of one who is self-conscious be described?

10. What in general would the objective symptoms of self-consciousness include?

11. Who is the Italian physiologist who gave us a classic description of self-consciousness and recovery from it?

12. What three divisions may be made of the state of self-consciousness?

13. Even though we cannot get at the exact physiological disturbance in self-consciousness, what in general happens to our nerves in this state?

14. What is meant by the chain of processes which lead to the result of an act, going on automatically in the lower centres?

QUESTIONNAIRE

15. What happens in self-consciousness in respect to these automatically working lower centres which carry out our acts?

16. What is the relationship between self-consciousness and mastery of a subject?

17. What is the relationship between self-consciousness and fear?

18. What is the hypothesis to explain the part of the body that might condition the experience of self-consciousness.

19. Does one or more causes produce self-consciousness?

20. What principal type of individual is subject to self-consciousness?

21. What two general types are, therefore, pitted against each other in respect to self-consciousness?

22. Is the demarcation line between the introvert and the extravert absolute and definite?

23. What is the difference in imagination between the self-conscious and the non-self-conscious individual?

24. How does the self-conscious individual impress one in regard to experience of the world?

25. Which of the four traditional temperaments, the sanguine, the phlegmatic, the choleric, and the melancholic, is given especially to self-consciousness?

26. Why do some connect self-consciousness with the build of the body, or the way it is constituted?

27. What is meant by the cyclothymic being less susceptible to self-consciousness?

28. What is meant by the cyclothymic being less susceptible to it?

29. In what way may glands have anything to do with self-consciousness?

30. How are those who are hypodynamic and hyperdynamic related to experiencing self-consciousness?

31. Why may it be thought that self-consciousness is a matter of self-submission?

QUESTIONNAIRE

32. Is a lack of self-confidence the basis of self-consciousness?

33. How do the British compare with other nations in regard to self-consciousness?

34. May it be that self-consciousness is a Gallic characteristic, or a trait of the Mediterranean people, who are very imaginative and emotional, such as the French and the Italians?

35. Who are some of the very famous writers mentioned in the present work that experienced self-consciousness?

36. May one be self-conscious in all public situations?

37. What compensating grace in a cultural way comes to one who is self-conscious?

38. What is meant by self-consciousness being a temporary but necessary stage?

39. What are some of the characteristics of the morbidly or very acutely self-conscious?

40. What was the delusion in the case of M. O'B., as recited in the text; and of many like her?

41. How may one be deluded in self-consciousness by ascribing mental brilliancy to others?

42. What is meant by saying that self-consciousness may border on paranoia?

43. How many general sets of causes are there for self-consciousness?

44. What is meant by the circumstantial cause setting off the basic or hereditary cause of self-consciousness?

45. What is meant by the momentary occasion setting off the basic or hereditary cause?

46. What distinction does the writer make between the efficient and the circumstantial cause?

47. How may these three sets of causes overlap?

QUESTIONNAIRE

48. What is the relationship between awkwardness and self-consciousness?

49. What kinds of intellect may be subject to self-consciousness?

50. What is the self-conscious equation?

51. Does a lack of self-confidence always indicate an intellectual insufficiency?

52. How is self-consciousness connected with the idea of giving oneself credit for performance?

53. Why do many speak of conditioning as a cause of self-consciousness?

54. What is the conclusion of the writer in respect to the hereditary cause of self-consciousness?

55. What is McDougall's recent explanation in regard to this theory?

56. What is meant by the dynamic theories of self-consciousness?

57. How does the writer refute the idea that organic weakness is the cause of self-consciousness?

58. What is the writer's opinion of the view that the malfunctioning of the endocrine glands is the cause of self-consciousness?

59. May self-consciousness depend upon a chemical alteration in one's organism?

60. What is meant by one's self-consciousness being a functional trouble?

61. According to this theory, is one who is self-conscious entirely submissive?

62. What is meant by self-consciousness being a compensatory fantasy?

63. How does the writer treat the inferiority feeling doctrine as being the basis of the state of nervousness?

64. How does the writer deal with the idea that self-consciousness is a matter of a guilt complex?

65. How does the writer treat the view that blushing is a matter of guilty feeling?

66. What are some of the handicaps of self-consciousness in daily life?

QUESTIONNAIRE

67. How should a manager of people conduct himself in regard to self-consciousness?

68. What is the wisdom of taking the "bull by the horns" and arbitrarily breaking through self-consciousness?

69. How is self-consciousness related to the extent of one's social contacts?

70. What is a compensation for self-consciousness in forcing oneself to be alone?

71. What, in summation, is the wrong attitude of mind of the self-conscious individual?

72. What is the relationship between achievement and self-consciousness?

73. Can self-consciousness be ultimately and definitely overcome?

74. What has sympathy to do with one's self-consciousness?

75. What may be said to be the besetting sin of self-consciousness?

76. Is it at all true that selfishness and self-consciousness go together?

77. Until one achieves a highly successful stage of life, what in the meantime should one do to overcome his self-consciousness?

78. Are we to understand that self-consciousness is to be suddenly eliminated?

79. Have proper diet and proper hygiene very much to do with curing self-consciousness?

80. Do stimulants aid in the elimination of self-consciousness?

81. Can self-consciousness be reduced by criticising others?

82. When may this remedy be resorted to?

83. What exercises are suggested for public performers to overcome the handicap of embarrassment?

84. Are sedatives to be taken as a cure for self-consciousness?

85. Does smoking help self-consciousness?

86. How much should one depend upon artificial methods to prevent self-consciousness?

QUESTIONNAIRE

87. Is it possible to experiment with self-consciousness?

88. What is meant by using non-social stimuli to study the extent of one's self-consciousness?

89. What is meant by a social passive situation to study self-consciousness?

90. What is meant by a social active situation to study self-consciousness?

91. Name some of the expressive methods in experimenting on emotional behavior.

92. How satisfactory are they?

93. Would you consider yourself self-conscious in a marked degree?

94. Have you observed any close relatives of yours or friends that are or were self-conscious?

95. If self-conscious, in what manner does this trouble manifest itself in your behavior?

96. If not self-conscious, describe your attitude toward those who show marked self-consciousness.

97. Since reading this book have you noticed any change in attitude or frame of mind?

98. Would you prefer not to have been troubled with self-consciousness?

99. Do you think that a time will come when self-consciousness will be entirely a thing of the past?

100. It has been said that immigrants are inclined to be self-conscious; How true is this? Would this apply to all foreigners?

BIBLIOGRAPHY

BIBLIOGRAPHY

NOTE: Articles on self-consciousness from a philosophical point of view are enclosed in square brackets.

1. ADLER, A.—*Understanding Human Nature,* 1927.

2. BERMAN, L.—*The Glands Regulating Personality,* 1922.

3. BEKHTEREV (Bechterew), V. M.—"Die Errötungsangst." *Neurologisches Centralblatt,* 1897.

4. BEKHTEREV, V. M.—"Ueber die Verrichtungen der Thalami bei den Tieren und beim Menschen." *Virchows Archiv,* 1887.

5. BRUGMANS, H. J. F. W.—"Die Verlegenheit, ihre Erscheinungen und ihr konstitutioneller Grund." *Zeitsch f. Psychol.* 1919, vol. LXXXI.

6. BURGESS, T. H.—*The Physiology or Mechanism of Blushing* (London), 1837.

[247]

7. CAMPBELL, H.—*Flushing and Morbid Blushing; their Pathology and Treatment* (London), 1890.

8. CAMPBELL, H.—*"Morbid Blushing,"* in *Wood's Monographs.*

9. [ANON.]—"Can Self-Consciousness Be Cured?" *Outlook,* 1906, vol. LXXXIII, pp. 784-786.

10. CANNON, W. B.—*Bodily Changes in Pain, Hunger, Fear and Rage* (revised edition), 1929.

11. CHARTERS, S.—*An Essay on Bashfulness* (London), 1836.

12. [CUNNINGHAM, G. W.—"Self-Consciousness and Consciousness of Self." *Mind,* 1911 (N.S.), vol. XX.]

13. DARWIN, C.—*The Expression of the Emotions in Man and Animals,* 1873.

14. DUGAS, L. M.—*La Timidité,* 1898 (in French).

15. DUGAS, L. M.—"La Pudeur: étude psychologique,'. *Rev. Philos,* 1903, vol. LVI.

16. DUGAS, L. M.—"La Timidité et l'Age." *Jour. de Psychol.,* 1915, vol. XII.

BIBLIOGRAPHY

17. DUGAS, L. M.—*Les Grands Timides*, 1922.

18. DUGAS, L. M.—Les Timides dans la Littérature et dans l'Art, 1925.

19. DUGAS, L. M.—"Qu'est ce que la Timidité?" *Psychol. et la Vie*, 1931, vol. V.

20. DUPUIS, L.—"Les Conditions biologiques de la timidité." *Rev. Philos.*, 1912, vol. LXXIV.

21. DUPUIS, L.—"Les stigmates fondamentaux de la timidité." *Rev. Philos.*, 1915, vol. LXXIX.

22. FRANK, L. K.—"The Management of Tensions." *American Journal of Sociology*, vol. XXXIII, 1928.

23. FRENCH, F. C.—Group Self-Consciousness: A Stage in the Evolution of Mind." *Psychol. Rev.*, 1906, vol. XV.

24. FREUD, S.—"On Narcissism" in *Collected Papers*, vol. IV, 1925.

25. GERZON, A. — *Die Scham*, 1919 (Abhandlungen aus d. Gebiete der Sexualforschung, vol. I.)

26. GRAU, K. J.—Eitelkeit und Schamgefühl (in German), 1928.

27. HADFIELD, J. A.—*Psychology and Morals,* 1923.

28. HADFIELD, J. A.—"Self-Consciousness in the Child" in *Health and Psychology of the Child* (edited by E. S. Chesser), 1925.

29. HALL, G. S.—"A Study of Fears." *American Journal of Psychology,* 1897, vol. VII.

30. HALL, G. S. and T. L. SMITH—"Showing Off and Bashfulness as Phases of Self-Consciousness." *Pedag. Seminary,* 1903. vol. X.

31. HARTENBERG, P.—Les Timides et la Timidité 1901, (4th revised edition, 1921).

32. HELLPACH, W.—"Vom Ausdruck der Verlegenheit." *Archiv. f.d. gesamte Psychol.* 1913, vol. XI.

33. HOHENEMSER, R.—"Versuch einer Analyse der Scham." *Archiv. f. d. gesamte Psychol.,* 1904, vol II.

34. JANET, PIERRE—*Les Obsessions et la Psychasthenie,* 1903.

35. KAHN, E.—*Psychopathic Personalities* (translated from the German), 1931.

BIBLIOGRAPHY

36. LAIRD, D. A.—*More Zest for Life*, 1935.

37. MacCURDY, J. T.—*The Psychology of Emotion, Morbid and Normal*, 1925.

38. McDOUGALL, WM.—*An Introduction to Social Psychology*, 1908.

39. MÉLINAND, C. — "Psychologie de la pudeur." *Revue d. Rev.*, 1901, ser. 3, vol. XXXVII.

40. MOSSO, A. — *Fear* translated from the Italian), 1896.

41. PARTRIDGE, G. E. — "Blushing." *Pedag Seminary*, 1897, vol. IV.

42. PITRES, A. and E. REGIS—"L'Obsession de la Rougeur." *Congrès des aliénistes et neurologistes* (Nancy), 1897.

43. PLUTARCH—"On Bashfulness" in his *Moralia* (translated from the Greek).

44. RIBOT, T.—*La Psychologie des Sentiments.*

45. RIGGS, A. F.—"Nervousness, Its Cause and Prevention." *Mental Hygiene*, vol. VI, 1922.

46. ROBACK, A. A.—*The Interference of Will Impulses.* Psychological Monographs, 1918 no. 111.

47. ROBACK, A. A.—*Personality: The Crux of Social Intercourse,* 1931.

48. ROBACK, A. A.—*Success in Handling Types* (pamphlet), 1935.

49. ROBACK, A. A.—*Overcoming Self-Consciousness and Other Inferiority Complexes* (pamphlet), 1936.

50. ROYCE, J.—"Some Observations on Anomalies of Self-Consciousness." *Psychol. Rev.,* 1935, vol. II (two articles).

51. SCHOUTEN, J.—*De Verlegenheid,* 1935 (in Dutch).

52. [SCOTT, W. H.—"Consciousness and Self-Consciousness." *Philos. Review,* 1918, vol. XXVII.]

53. SKIDELSKY, B. C.—"The Blight of Fear." *Nation's Health,* vol. IV, 1922.

54. TITCHENER, E. B. — "Consciousness of Self." *American Journal of Psychology,* 1911, vol. XXII.

55. TODD, J. A. — "Primitive Notions of the Self." *Amer. Jour. of Psychol.,* 1916, vol. XXVII.

BIBLIOGRAPHY

56. VENDELL, M. — "La timidez en los niños Cubanos." *Revista de la facultad de letras y ciencias* (Habana), 1921 (in Spanish).

57. VOIGTLAENDER, Else — *Vom Selbstegefühl,* 1910 (in German).

58. WALSH, W. S.—*The Mastery of Fear,* 1924.

59. WILLIAMS, T. A.—*Dreads and Besetting Fears,* 1923.

60. WITTELS, F.—"Narcissism" in *Sex in Civilization,* 1929.

61. [WRIGHT, H. W.—"Natural Selection and Self-Conscious Development." *Philos. Review,* 1905, vol. XIV.]

INDEXES

REGISTER OF NAMES

(Note: Names and Characters in fiction or mythology appear in bold type.)

REGISTER OF NAMES

[258]

INDEX OF SUBJECTS

INDEX OF SUBJECTS

INDEX OF SUBJECTS

INDEX OF SUBJECTS